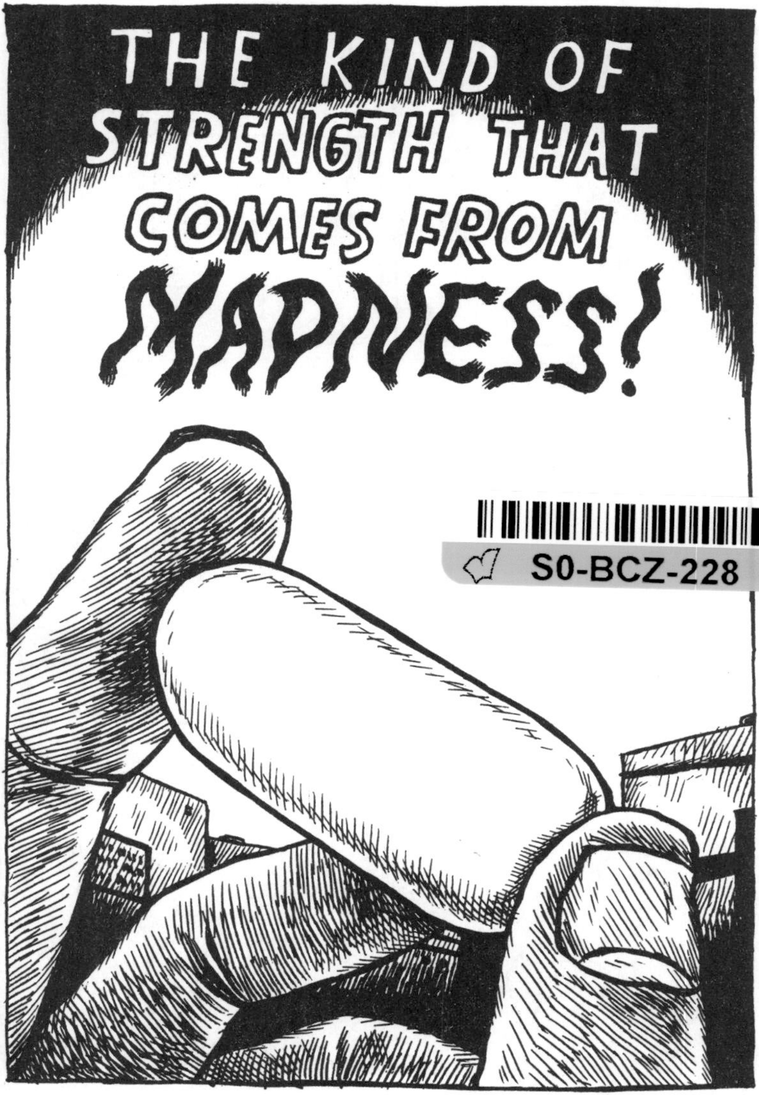
THE KIND OF
STRENGTH THAT
COMES FROM
MADNESS!

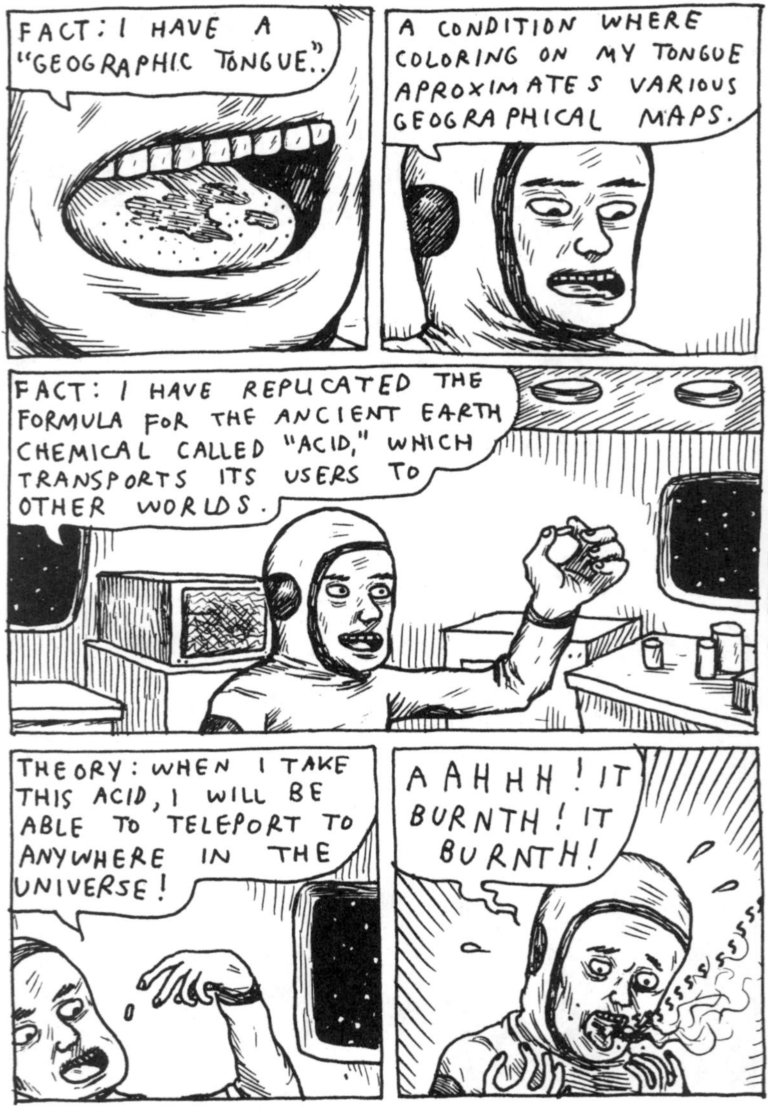
FACT: I HAVE A "GEOGRAPHIC TONGUE."
A CONDITION WHERE COLORING ON MY TONGUE APROXIMATES VARIOUS GEOGRAPHICAL MAPS.
FACT: I HAVE REPLICATED THE FORMULA FOR THE ANCIENT EARTH CHEMICAL CALLED "ACID," WHICH TRANSPORTS ITS USERS TO OTHER WORLDS.
THEORY: WHEN I TAKE THIS ACID, I WILL BE ABLE TO TELEPORT TO ANYWHERE IN THE UNIVERSE!
AAHHH! IT BURNTH! IT BURNTH!
SSSSSSSSSS

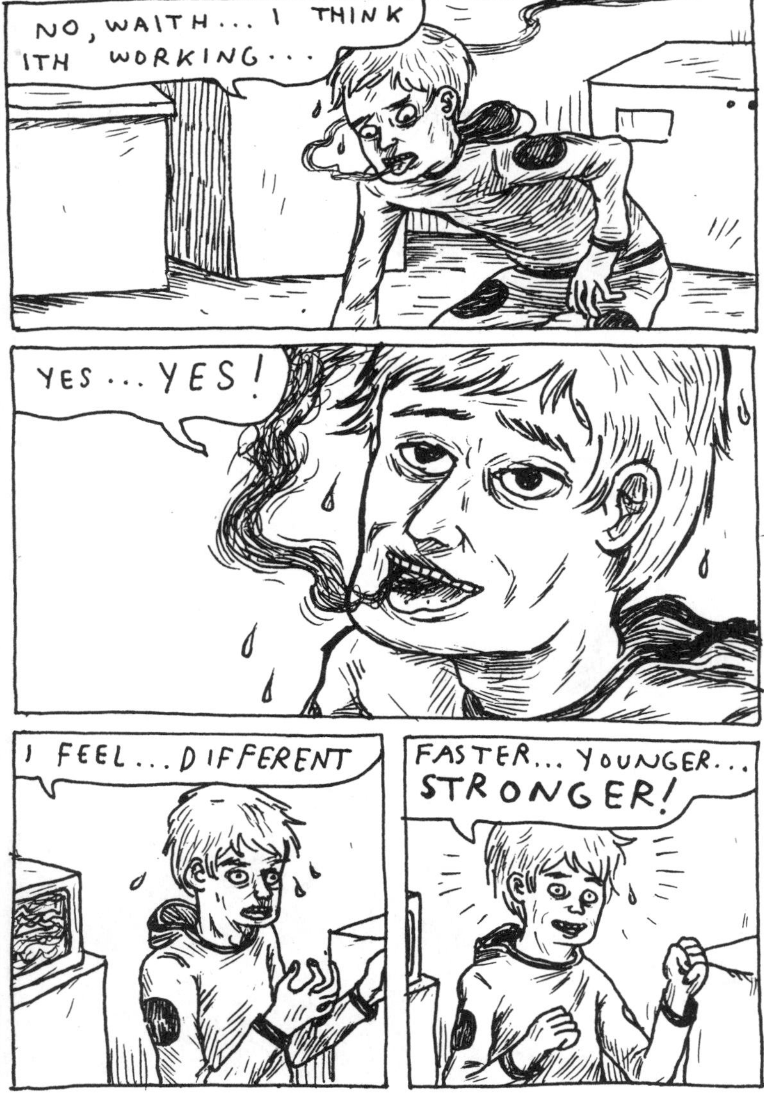
NO, WAITH... I THINK ITH WORKING...
YES... YES!
I FEEL... DIFFERENT
FASTER... YOUNGER... STRONGER!

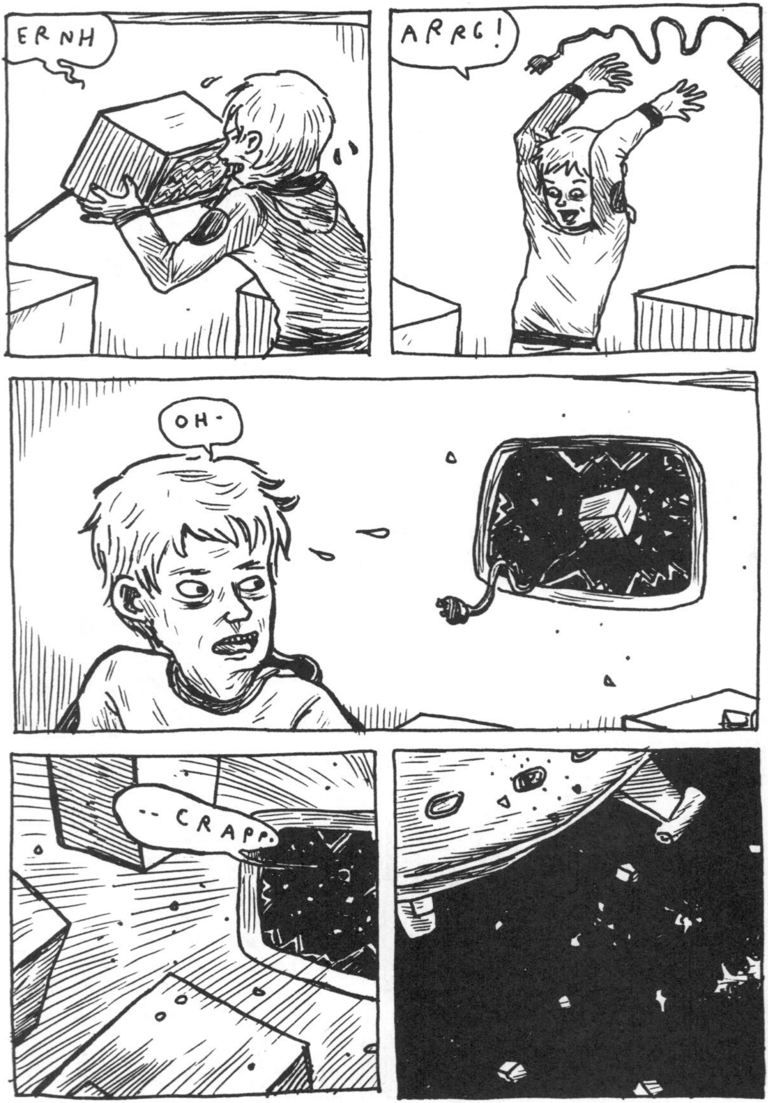
ERNH
ARRG!
OH-
-- CRAPP.

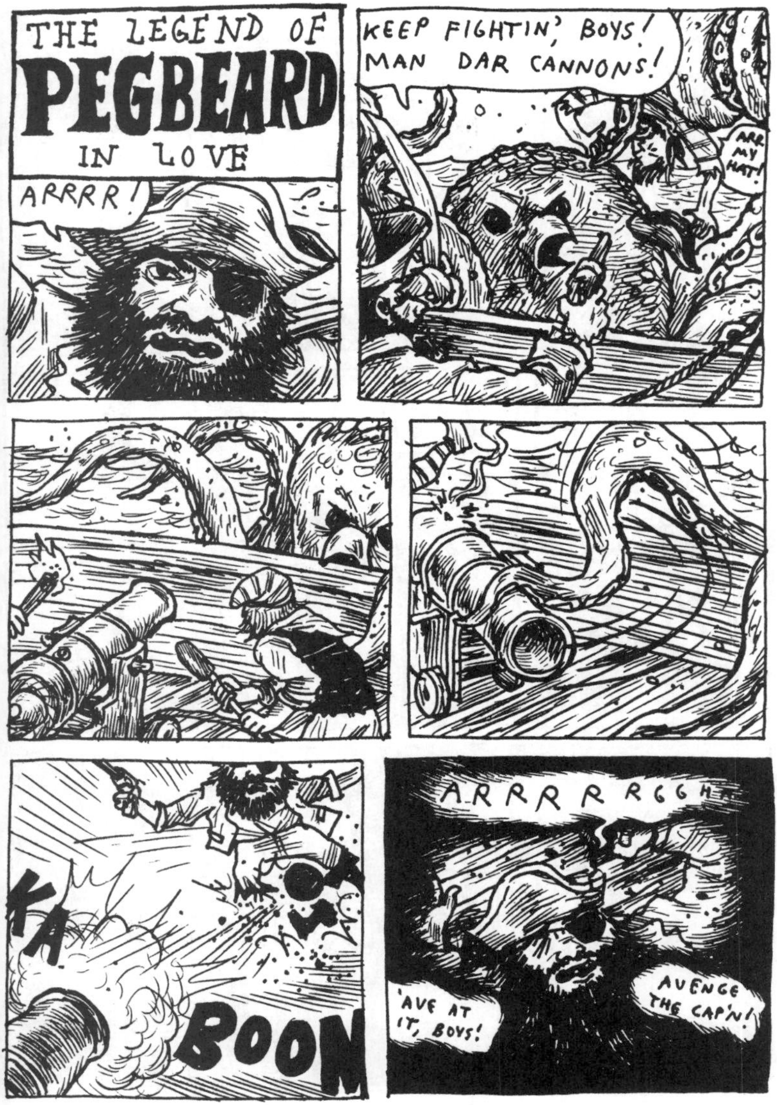
THE LEGEND OF
PEGBEARD
IN LOVE
ARRRR!
KEEP FIGHTIN', BOYS! MAN DAR CANNONS!
ARR MY HAT!
KA
BOOM
ARRRRRRGGH
'AVE AT IT, BOYS!
AVENGE THE CAP'N!

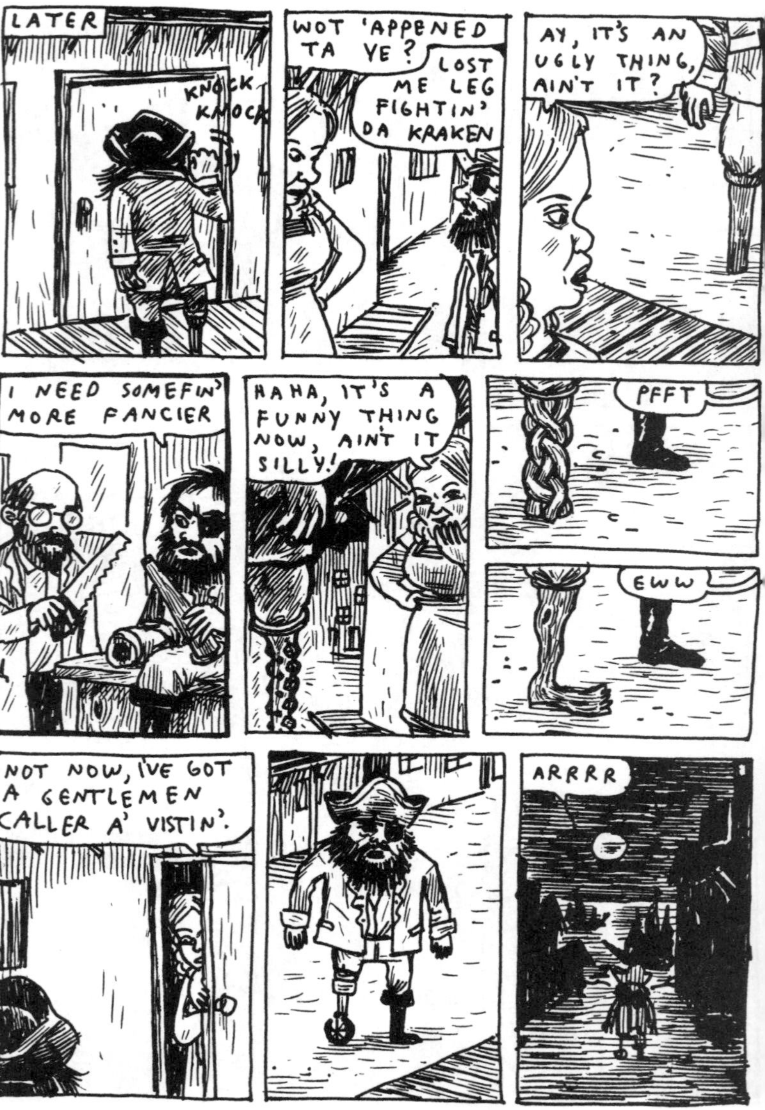
LATER
KNOCK KNOCK
WOT 'APPENED TA YE?
LOST ME LEG FIGHTIN' DA KRAKEN
AY, IT'S AN UGLY THING, AIN'T IT?
I NEED SOMEFIN' MORE FANCIER
HAHA, IT'S A FUNNY THING NOW, AINT IT SILLY!
PFFT
EWW
NOT NOW, I'VE GOT A GENTLEMEN CALLER A' VISTIN'.
ARRRR

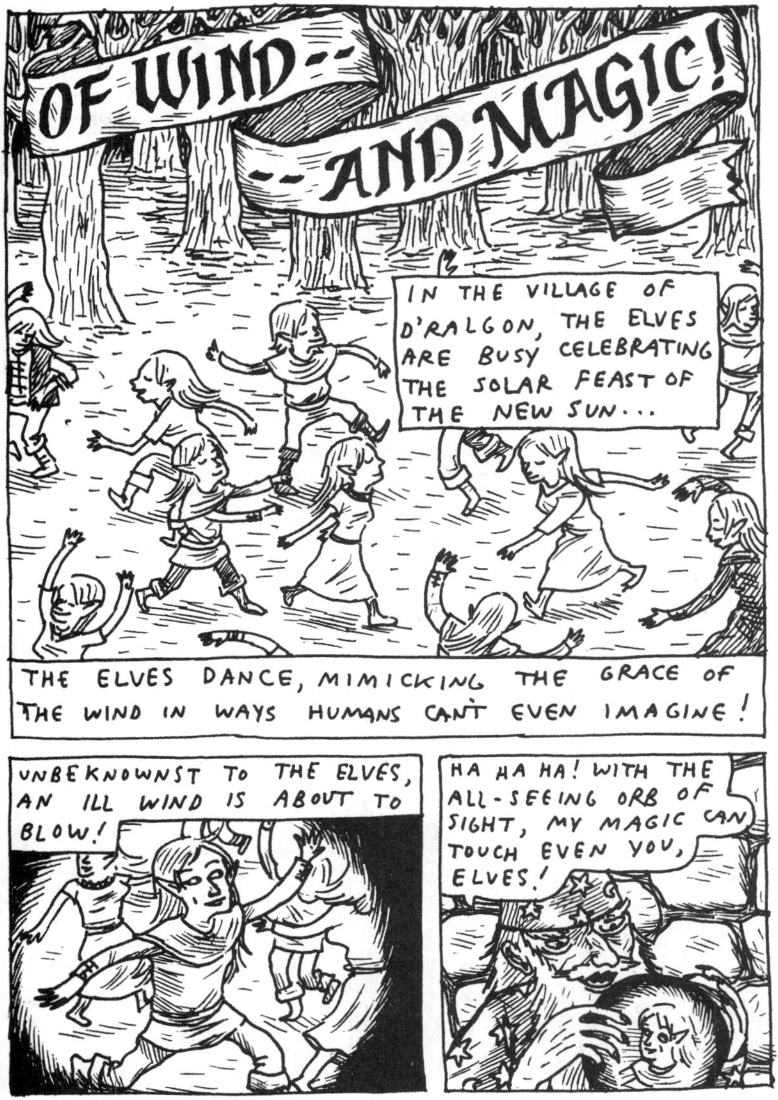
OF WIND--
--AND MAGIC!
IN THE VILLAGE OF D'RALGON, THE ELVES ARE BUSY CELEBRATING THE SOLAR FEAST OF THE NEW SUN...
THE ELVES DANCE, MIMICKING THE GRACE OF THE WIND IN WAYS HUMANS CAN'T EVEN IMAGINE!
UNBEKNOWNST TO THE ELVES, AN ILL WIND IS ABOUT TO BLOW!
HA HA HA! WITH THE ALL-SEEING ORB OF SIGHT, MY MAGIC CAN TOUCH EVEN YOU, ELVES!

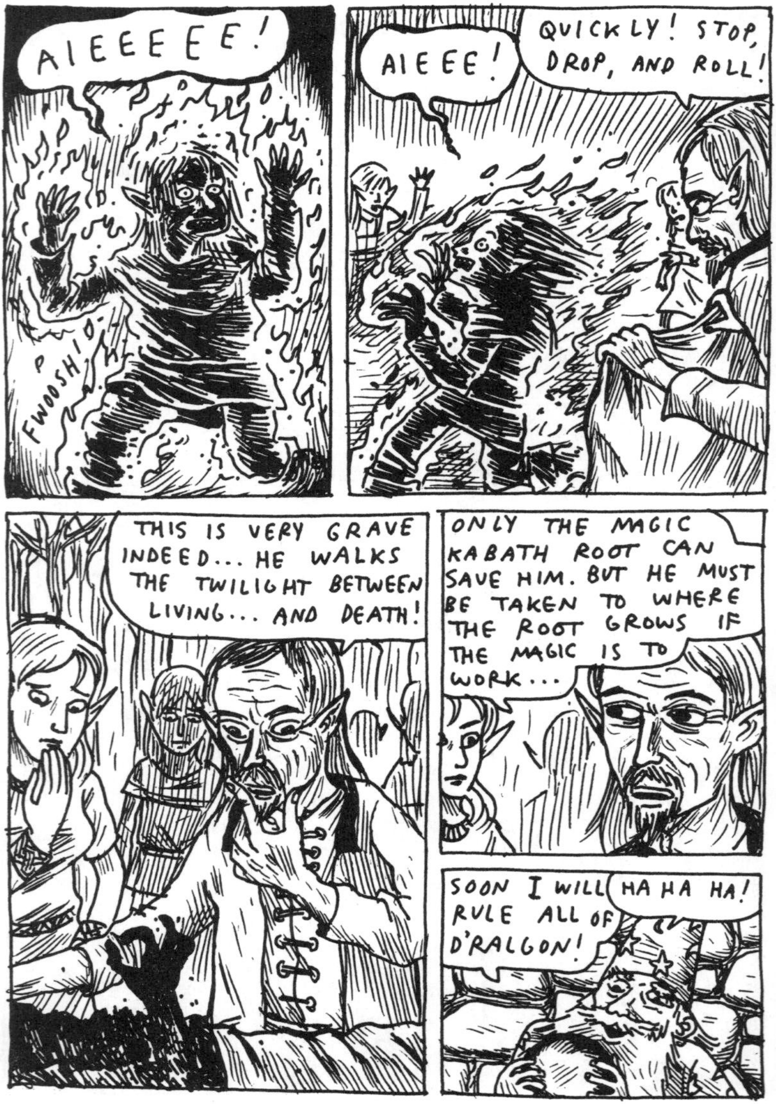
AIEEEEEE!
FWOOSH!
AIEEE!
QUICKLY! STOP, DROP, AND ROLL!
THIS IS VERY GRAVE INDEED... HE WALKS THE TWILIGHT BETWEEN LIVING... AND DEATH!
ONLY THE MAGIC KABATH ROOT CAN SAVE HIM. BUT HE MUST BE TAKEN TO WHERE THE ROOT GROWS IF THE MAGIC IS TO WORK...
SOON I WILL RULE ALL OF D'RALGON!
HA HA HA!

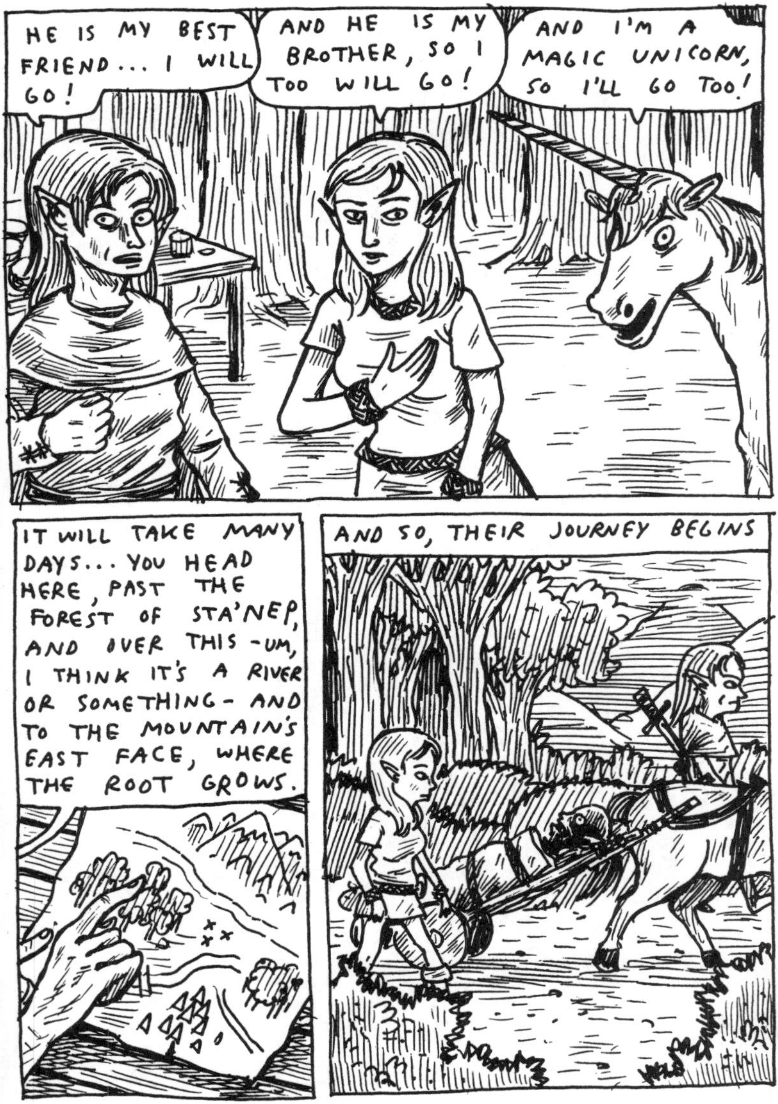
HE IS MY BEST FRIEND... I WILL GO!
AND HE IS MY BROTHER, SO I TOO WILL GO!
AND I'M A MAGIC UNICORN, SO I'LL GO TOO!
IT WILL TAKE MANY DAYS... YOU HEAD HERE, PAST THE FOREST OF STA'NEP, AND OVER THIS -UM, I THINK IT'S A RIVER OR SOMETHING- AND TO THE MOUNTAIN'S EAST FACE, WHERE THE ROOT GROWS.
AND SO, THEIR JOURNEY BEGINS

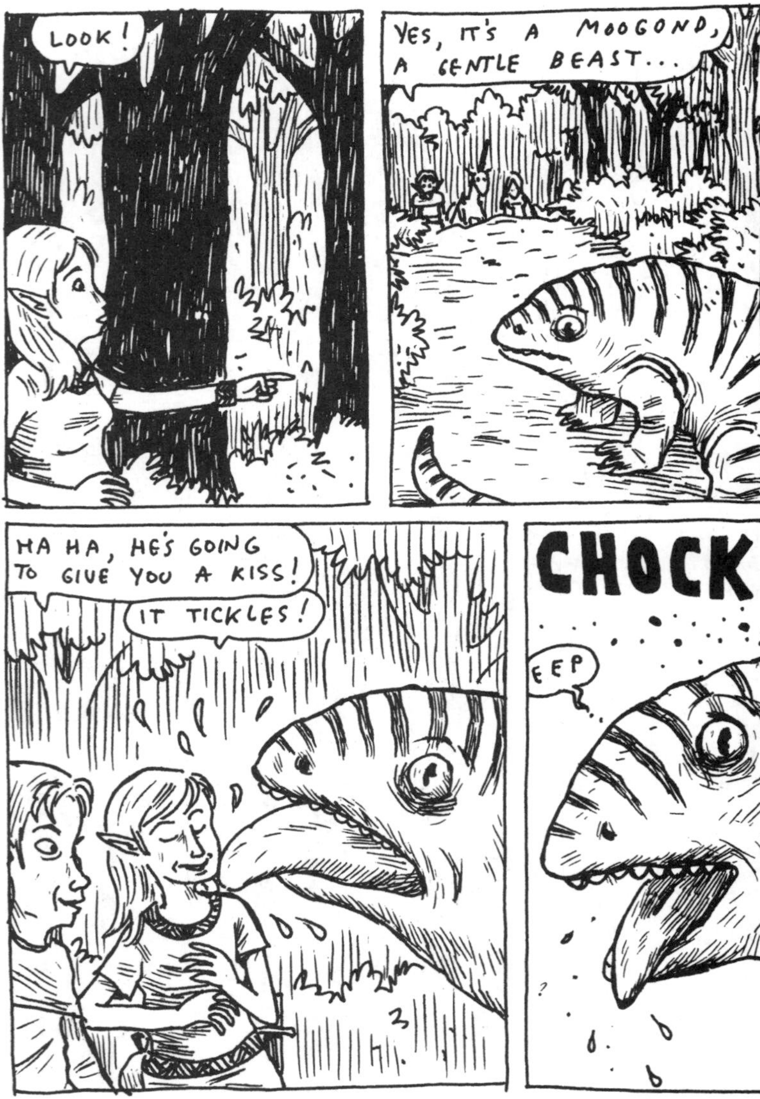
LOOK!
YES, IT'S A MOOGOND, A GENTLE BEAST...
HA HA, HE'S GOING TO GIVE YOU A KISS!
IT TICKLES!
CHOCK
EEP

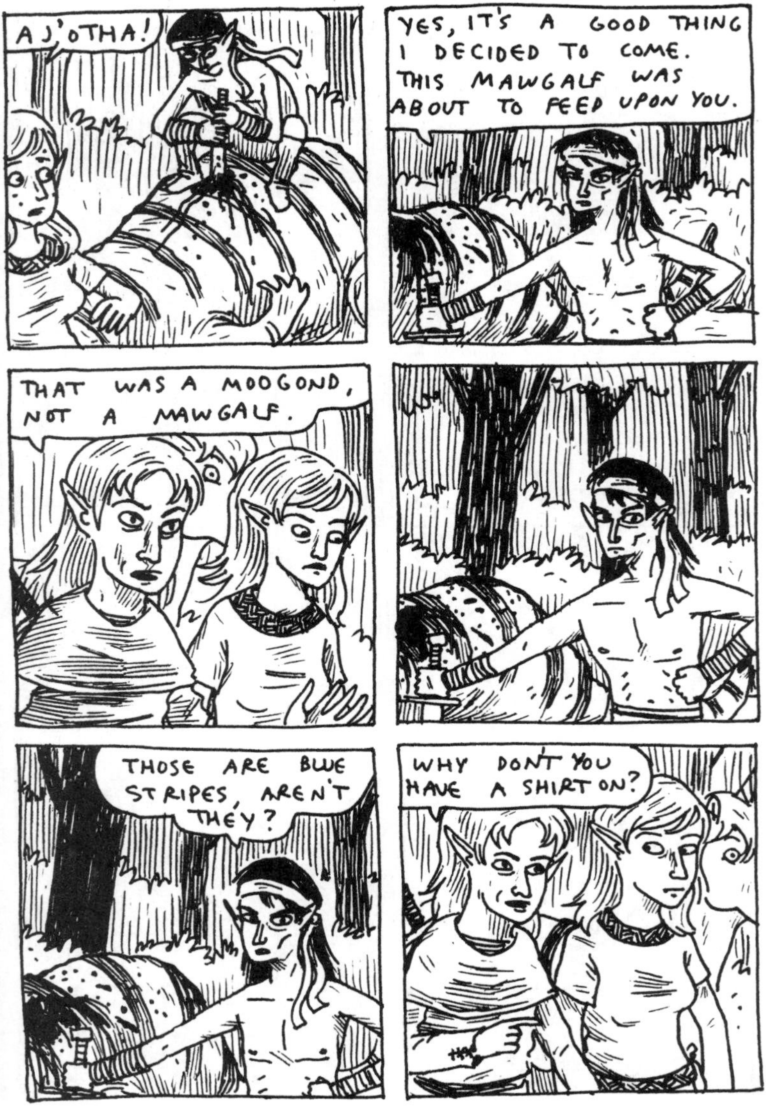
A J'OTHA!
YES, IT'S A GOOD THING I DECIDED TO COME. THIS MAWGALF WAS ABOUT TO FEED UPON YOU.
THAT WAS A MOOGOND, NOT A MAWGALF.
THOSE ARE BLUE STRIPES, AREN'T THEY?
WHY DON'T YOU HAVE A SHIRT ON?

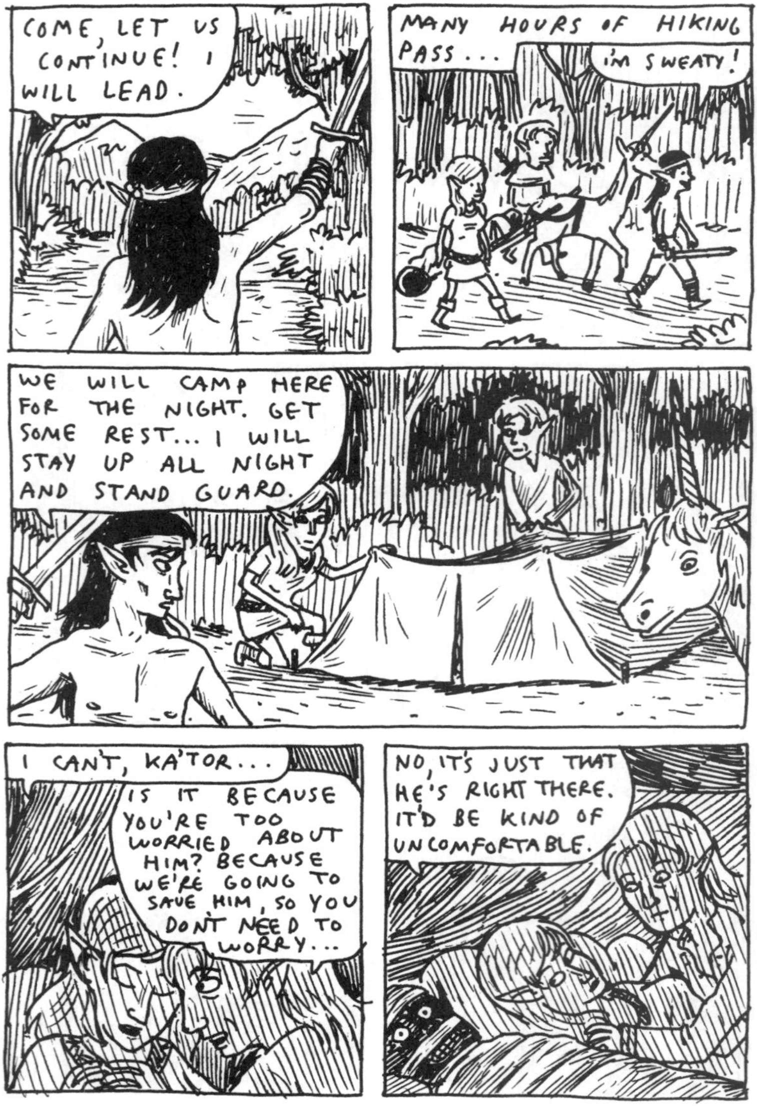
COME, LET US CONTINUE! I WILL LEAD.
MANY HOURS OF HIKING PASS...
I'M SWEATY!
WE WILL CAMP HERE FOR THE NIGHT. GET SOME REST... I WILL STAY UP ALL NIGHT AND STAND GUARD.
I CAN'T, KA'TOR...
IS IT BECAUSE YOU'RE TOO WORRIED ABOUT HIM? BECAUSE WE'RE GOING TO SAVE HIM, SO YOU DON'T NEED TO WORRY...
NO, IT'S JUST THAT HE'S RIGHT THERE. IT'D BE KIND OF UNCOMFORTABLE.

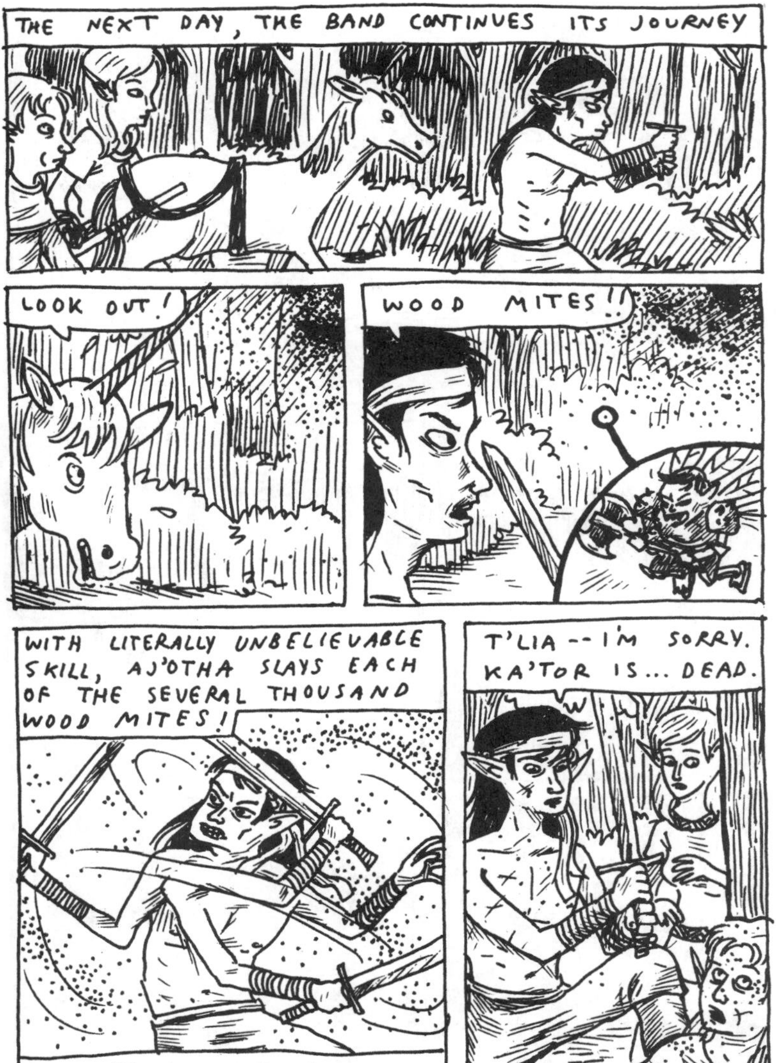
THE NEXT DAY, THE BAND CONTINUES ITS JOURNEY
LOOK OUT!
WOOD MITES!!
WITH LITERALLY UNBELIEVABLE SKILL, AJ'OTHA SLAYS EACH OF THE SEVERAL THOUSAND WOOD MITES!
HOWEVER, HE IS TOO SLOW...
T'LIA -- I'M SORRY. KA'TOR IS... DEAD.

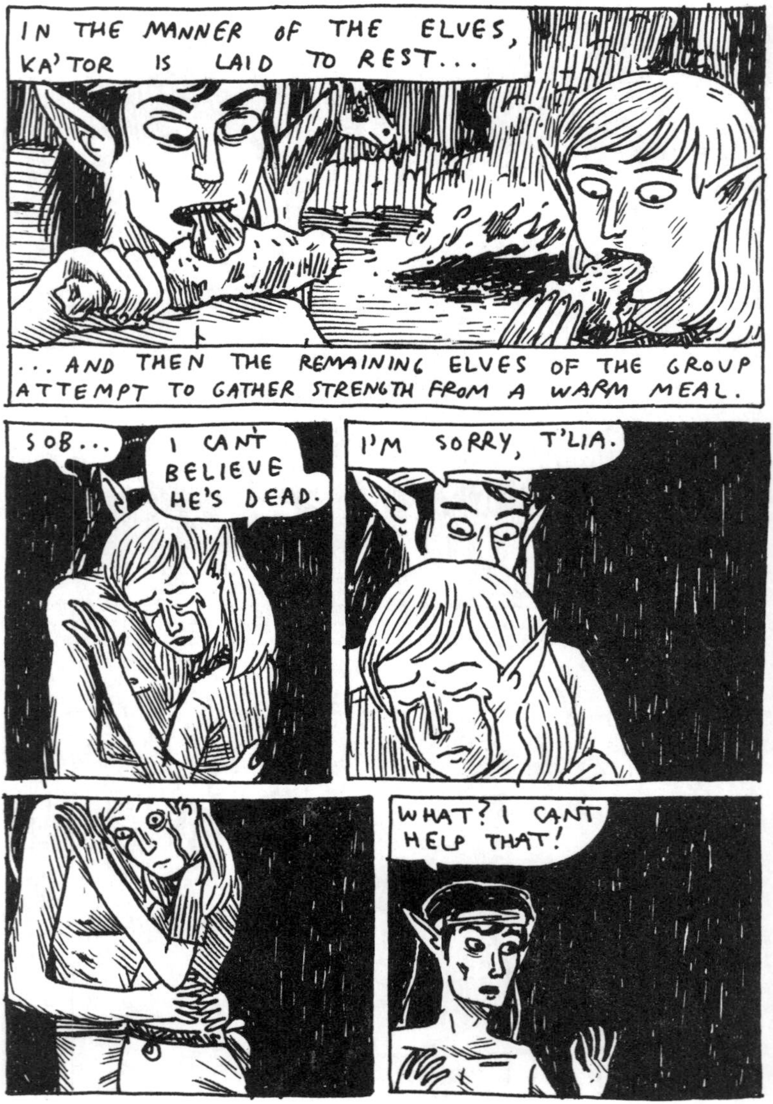
IN THE MANNER OF THE ELVES, KA'TOR IS LAID TO REST...
...AND THEN THE REMAINING ELVES OF THE GROUP ATTEMPT TO GATHER STRENGTH FROM A WARM MEAL.
SOB...
I CAN'T BELIEVE HE'S DEAD.
I'M SORRY, T'LIA.
WHAT? I CAN'T HELP THAT!

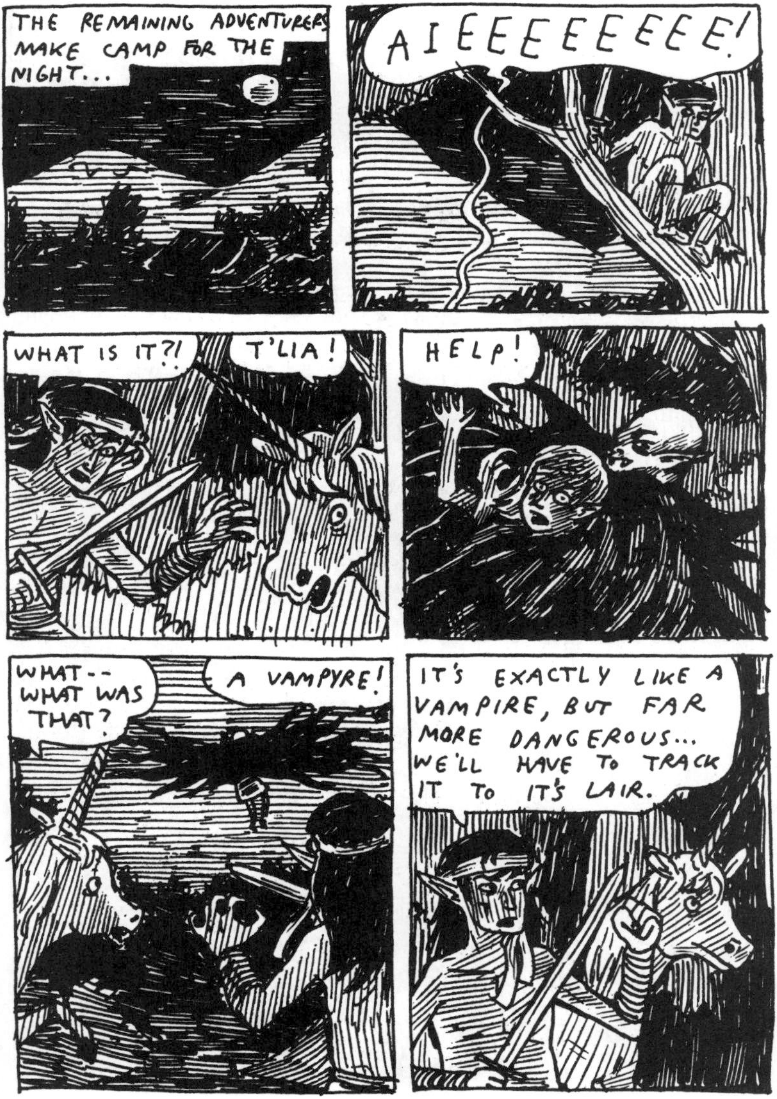
THE REMAINING ADVENTURERS MAKE CAMP FOR THE NIGHT...
AIEEEEEEEEE!
WHAT IS IT?!
T'LIA!
HELP!
WHAT-- WHAT WAS THAT?
A VAMPYRE!
IT'S EXACTLY LIKE A VAMPIRE, BUT FAR MORE DANGEROUS... WE'LL HAVE TO TRACK IT TO IT'S LAIR.

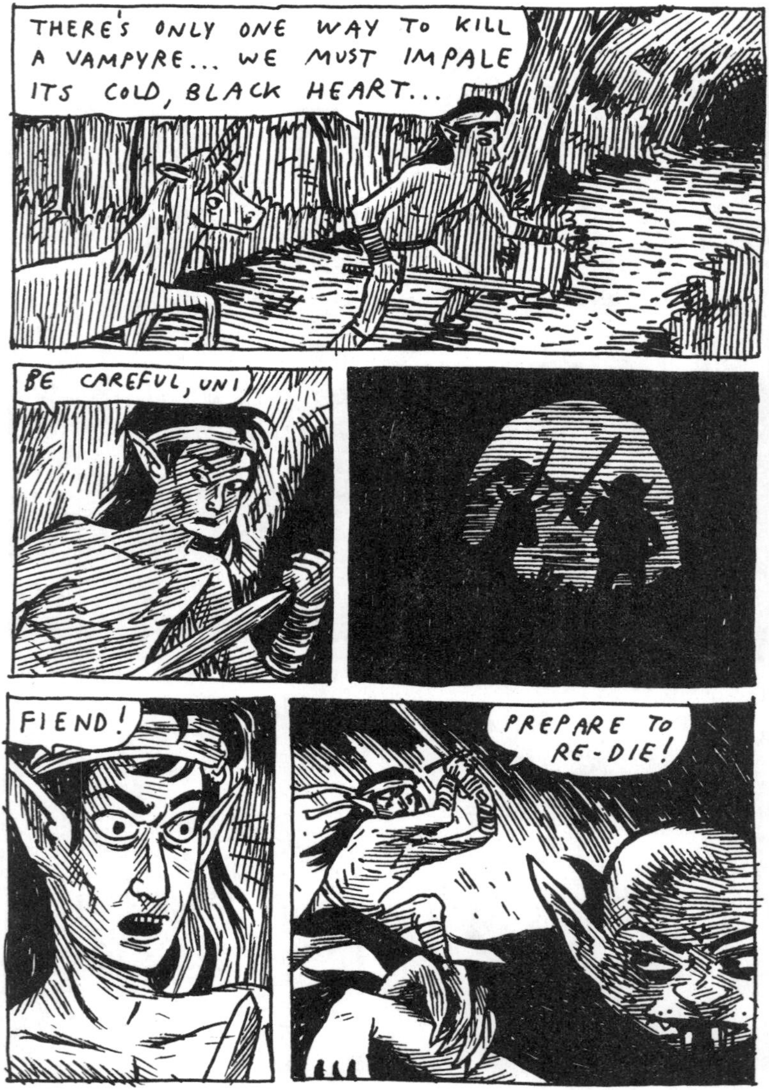
THERE'S ONLY ONE WAY TO KILL A VAMPYRE... WE MUST IMPALE ITS COLD, BLACK HEART...
BE CAREFUL, UNI
FIEND!
PREPARE TO RE-DIE!

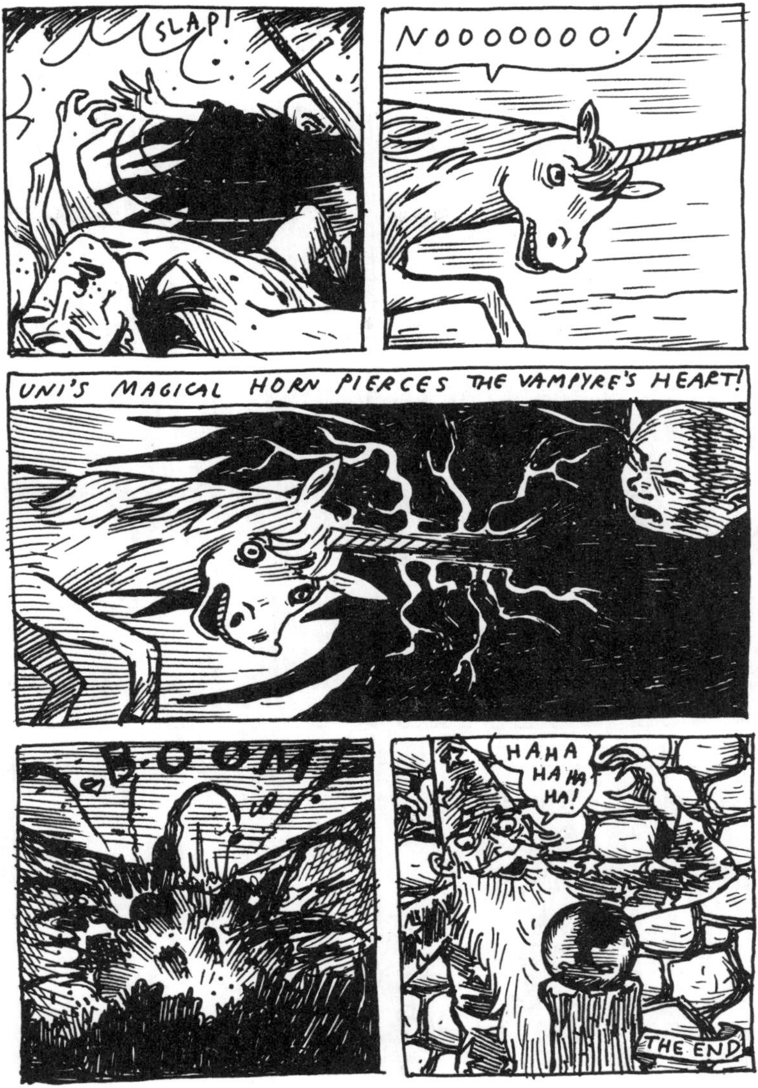
SLAP!
NOOOOOOO!
UNI'S MAGICAL HORN PIERCES THE VAMPYRE'S HEART!
BOOM!
HAHA HAHA HA!
THE END

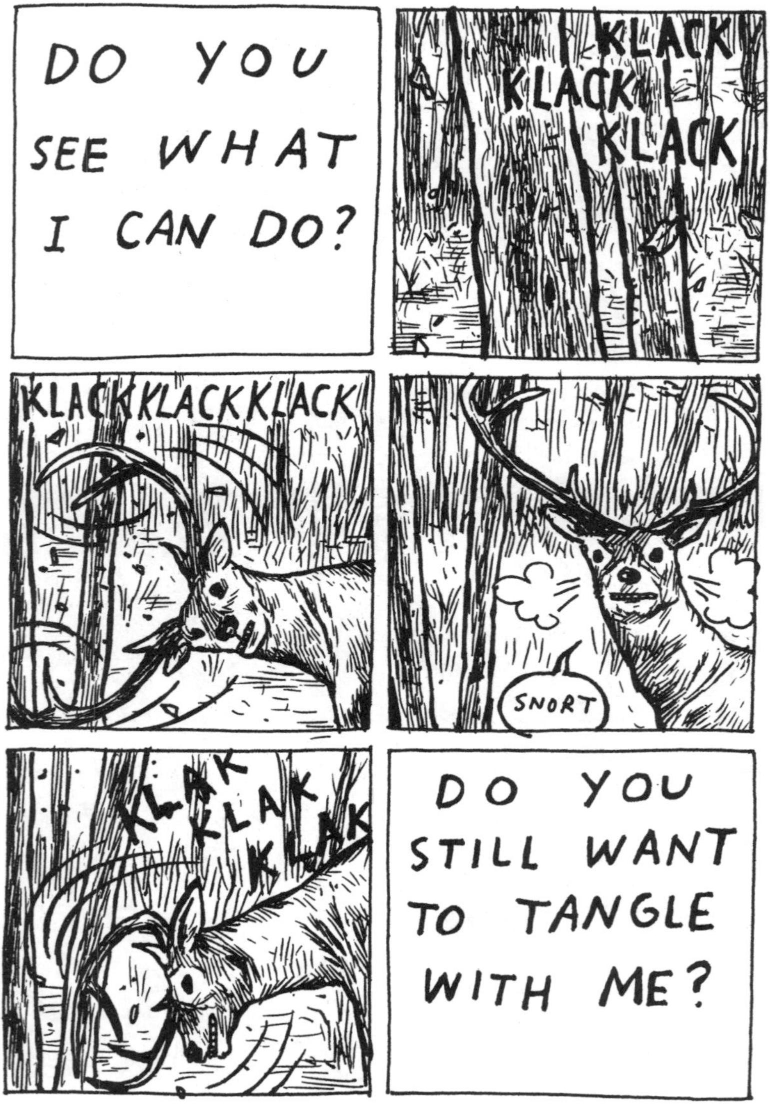
DO YOU SEE WHAT I CAN DO?
KLACK
KLACK
KLACK
KLACKKLACKKLACK
SNORT
KLAK
KLAK
KLAK
DO YOU STILL WANT TO TANGLE WITH ME?

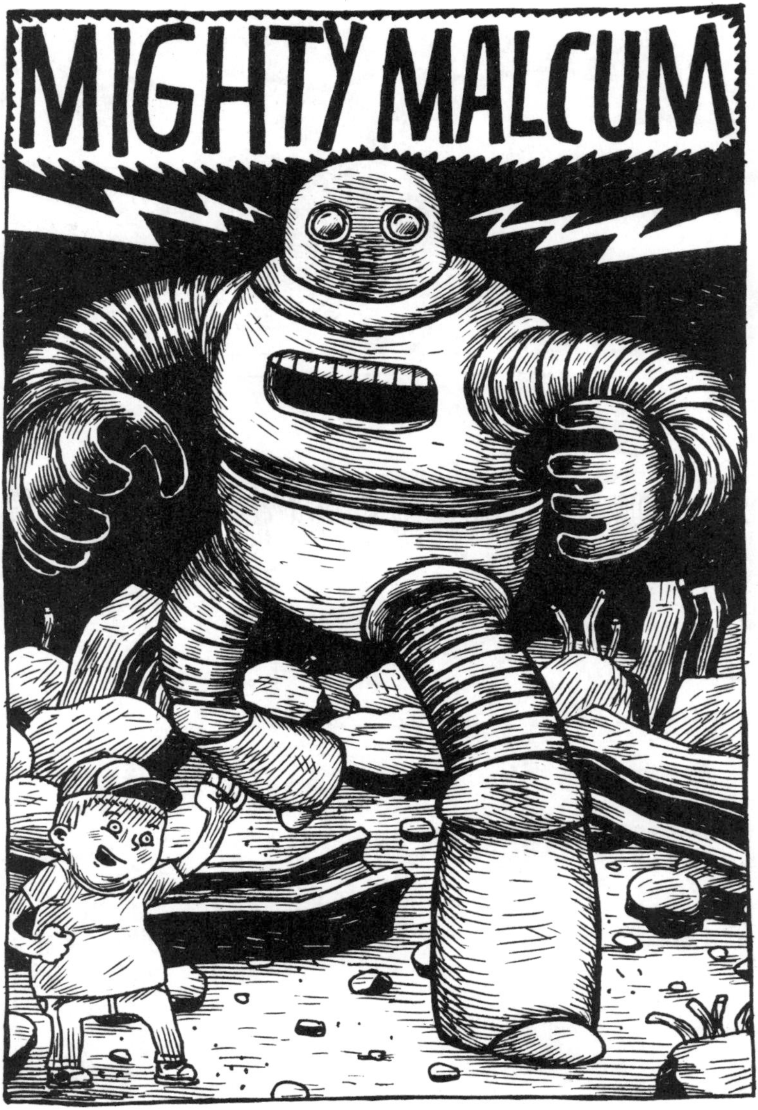
MIGHTY MALCUM

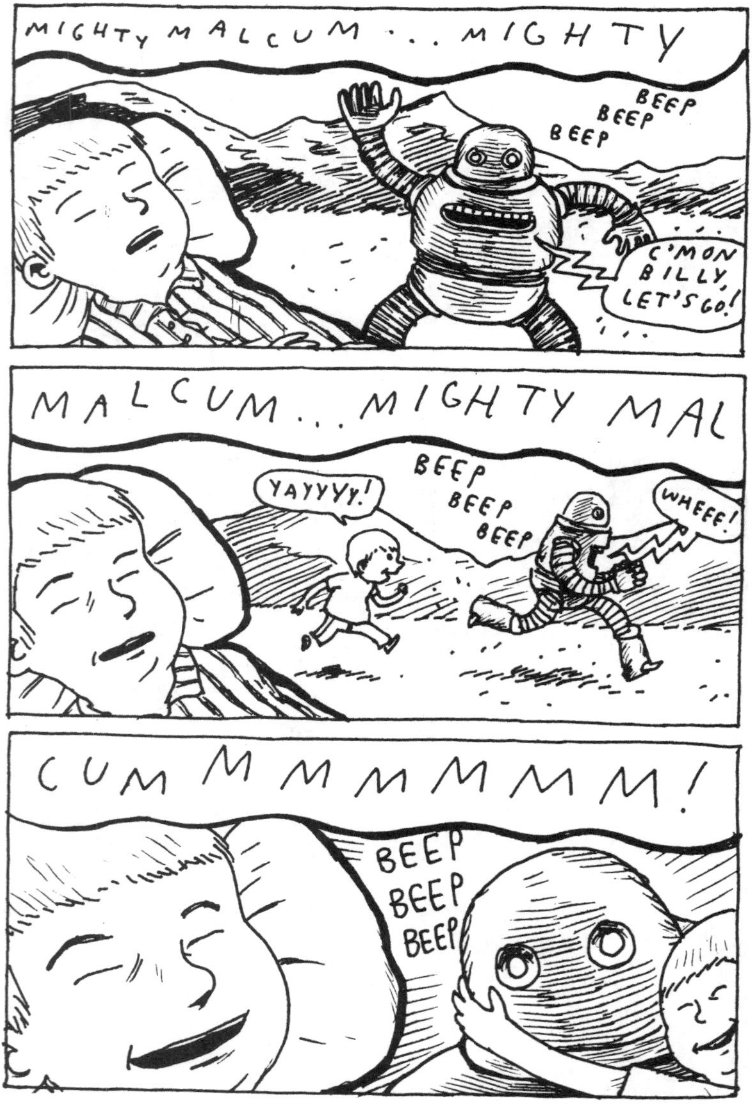
MIGHTY MALCUM ... MIGHTY
BEEP BEEP BEEP
C'MON BILLY, LET'S GO!
MALCUM... MIGHTY MAL
YAYYYY!
BEEP BEEP BEEP
WHEEE!
CUMMMMMMMM!
BEEP BEEP BEEP

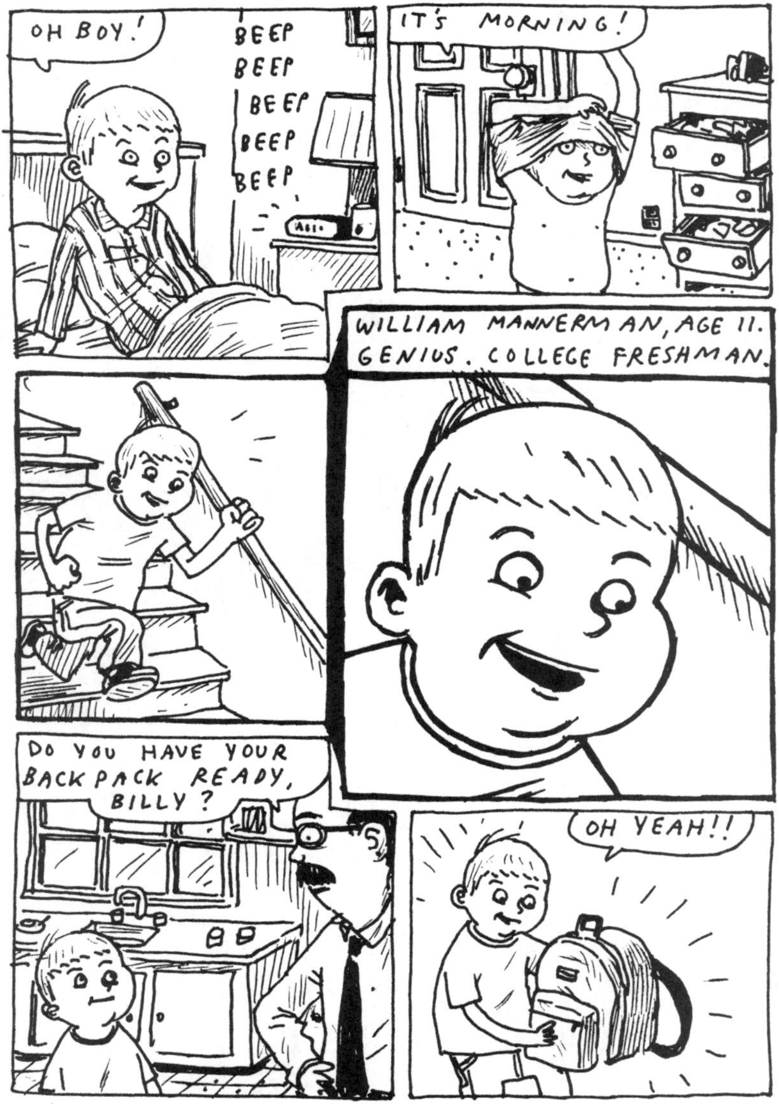
OH BOY!
BEEP
BEEP
BEEP
BEEP
BEEP
IT'S MORNING!
WILLIAM MANNERMAN, AGE 11. GENIUS. COLLEGE FRESHMAN.
DO YOU HAVE YOUR BACKPACK READY, BILLY?
OH YEAH!!

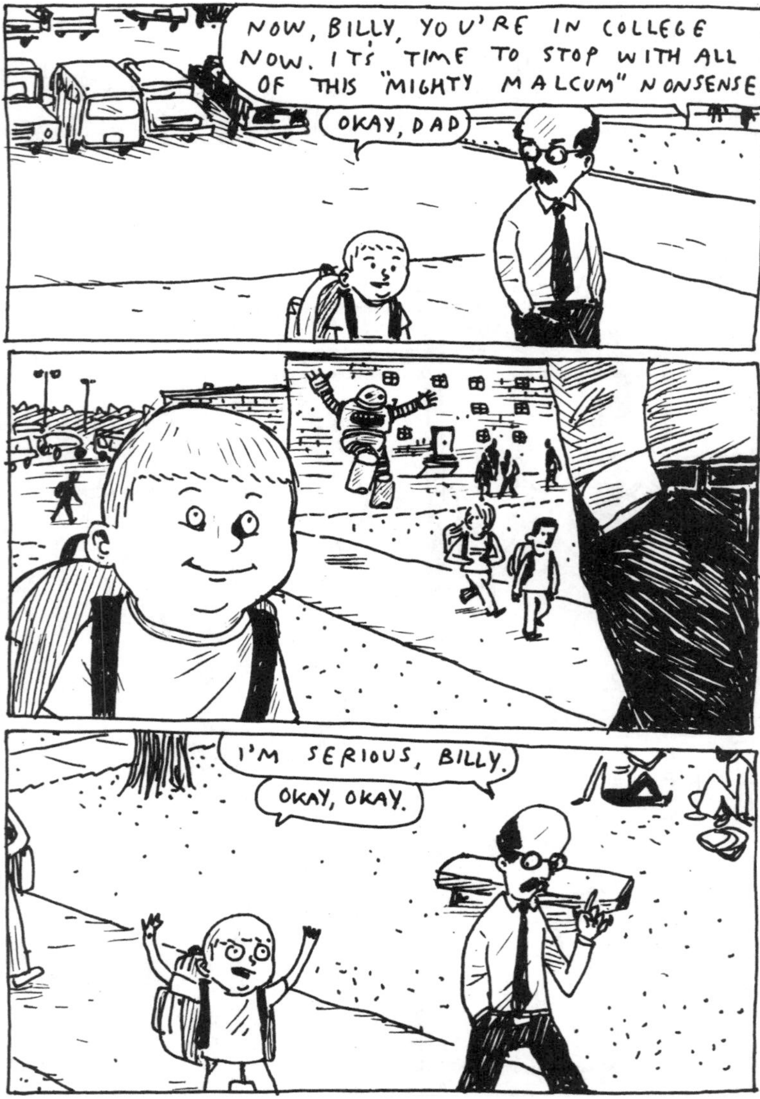
NOW, BILLY, YOU'RE IN COLLEGE NOW. IT'S TIME TO STOP WITH ALL OF THIS "MIGHTY MALCUM" NONSENSE.
OKAY, DAD
I'M SERIOUS, BILLY.
OKAY, OKAY.

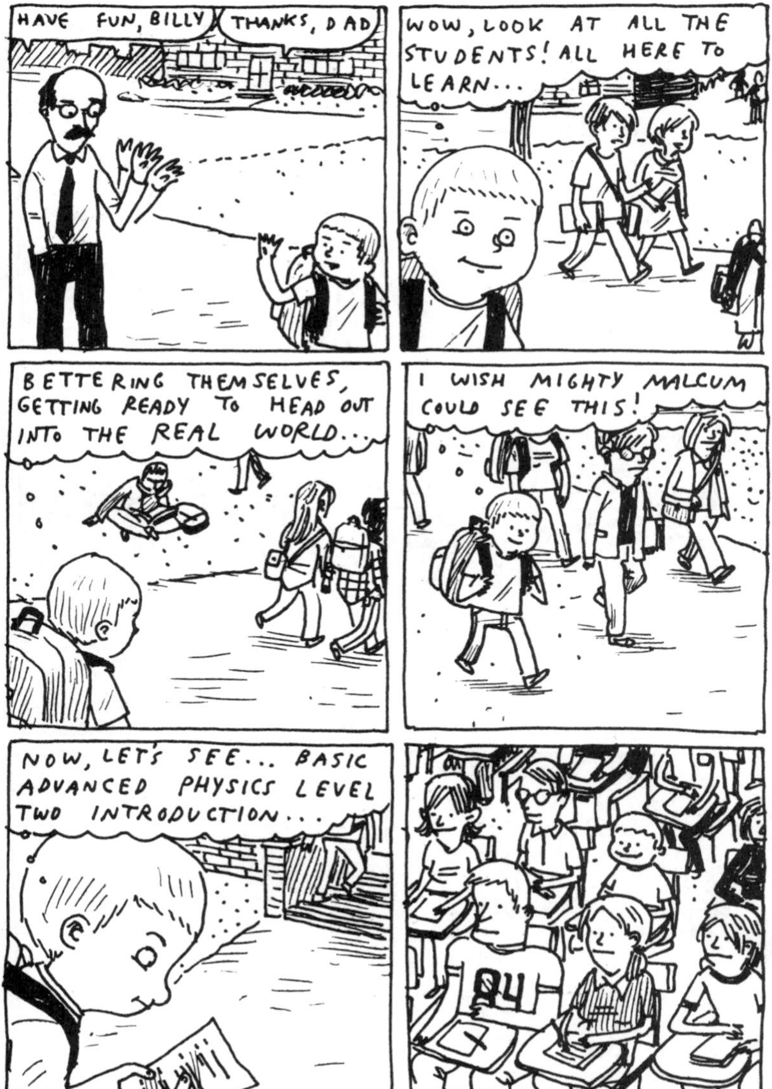
HAVE FUN, BILLY
THANKS, DAD
WOW, LOOK AT ALL THE STUDENTS! ALL HERE TO LEARN...
BETTERING THEMSELVES, GETTING READY TO HEAD OUT INTO THE REAL WORLD...
I WISH MIGHTY MALCUM COULD SEE THIS!
NOW, LET'S SEE... BASIC ADVANCED PHYSICS LEVEL TWO INTRODUCTION...
84

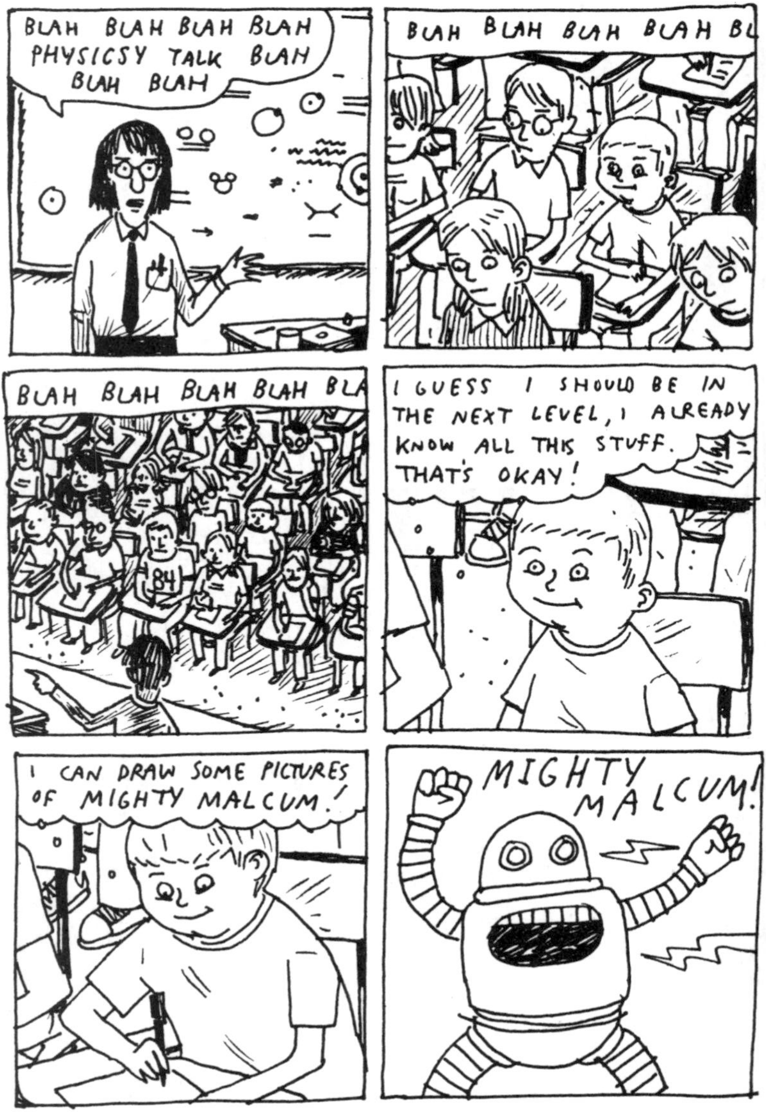
BLAH BLAH BLAH BLAH PHYSICSY TALK BLAH BLAH BLAH
BLAH BLAH BLAH BLAH BL
BLAH BLAH BLAH BLAH BLA
I GUESS I SHOULD BE IN THE NEXT LEVEL, I ALREADY KNOW ALL THIS STUFF. THAT'S OKAY!
84
I CAN DRAW SOME PICTURES OF MIGHTY MALCUM!
MIGHTY MALCUM!

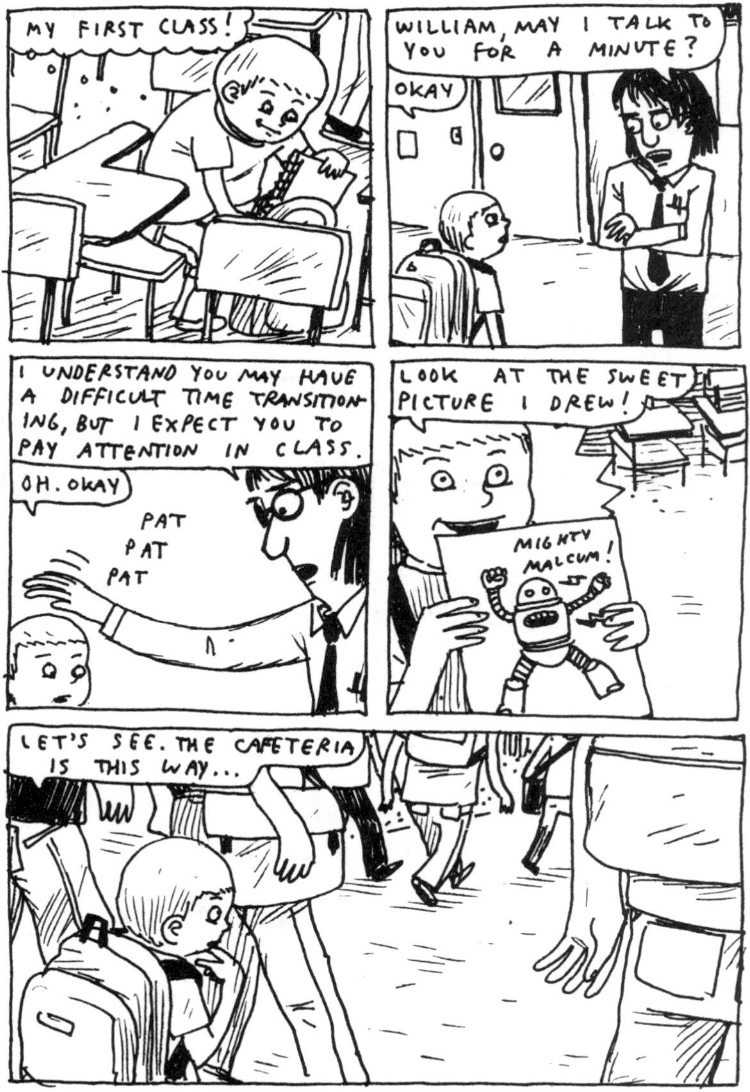
MY FIRST CLASS!
WILLIAM, MAY I TALK TO YOU FOR A MINUTE?
OKAY
I UNDERSTAND YOU MAY HAVE A DIFFICULT TIME TRANSITIONING, BUT I EXPECT YOU TO PAY ATTENTION IN CLASS.
OH. OKAY
PAT PAT PAT
LOOK AT THE SWEET PICTURE I DREW!
MIGHTY MALCUM!
LET'S SEE. THE CAFETERIA IS THIS WAY...

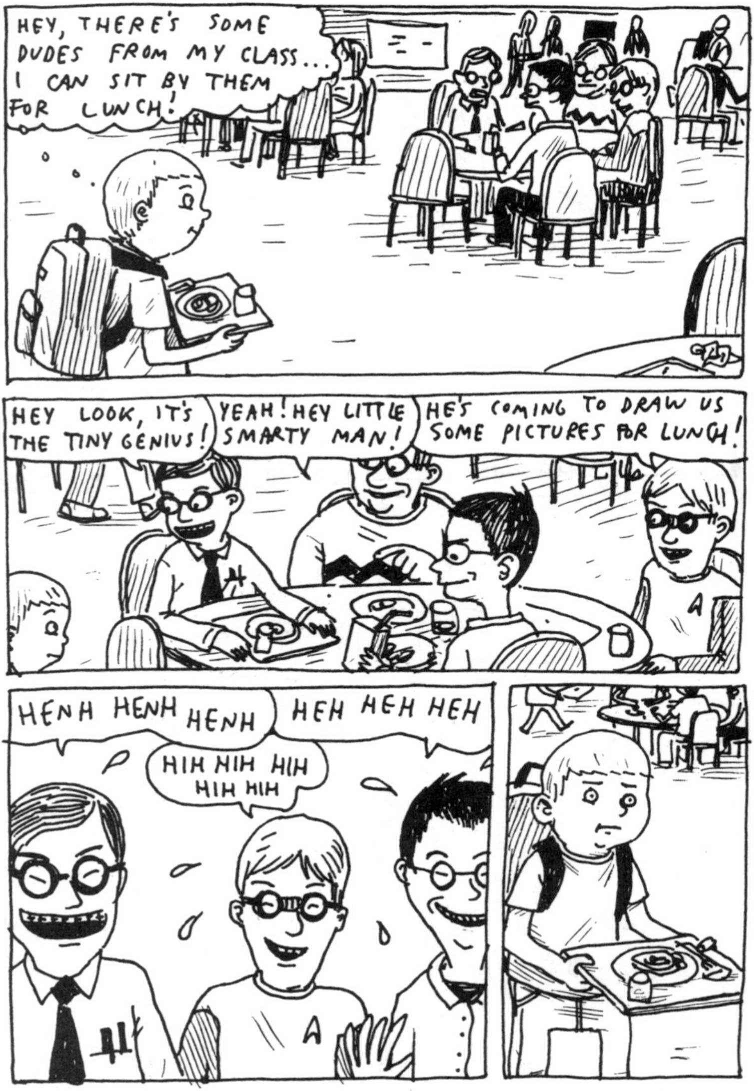
HEY, THERE'S SOME DUDES FROM MY CLASS... I CAN SIT BY THEM FOR LUNCH!
HEY LOOK, IT'S THE TINY GENIUS!
YEAH! HEY LITTLE SMARTY MAN!
HE'S COMING TO DRAW US SOME PICTURES FOR LUNCH!
HENH HENH HENH
HEH HEH HEH
HIH HIH HIH HIH HIH

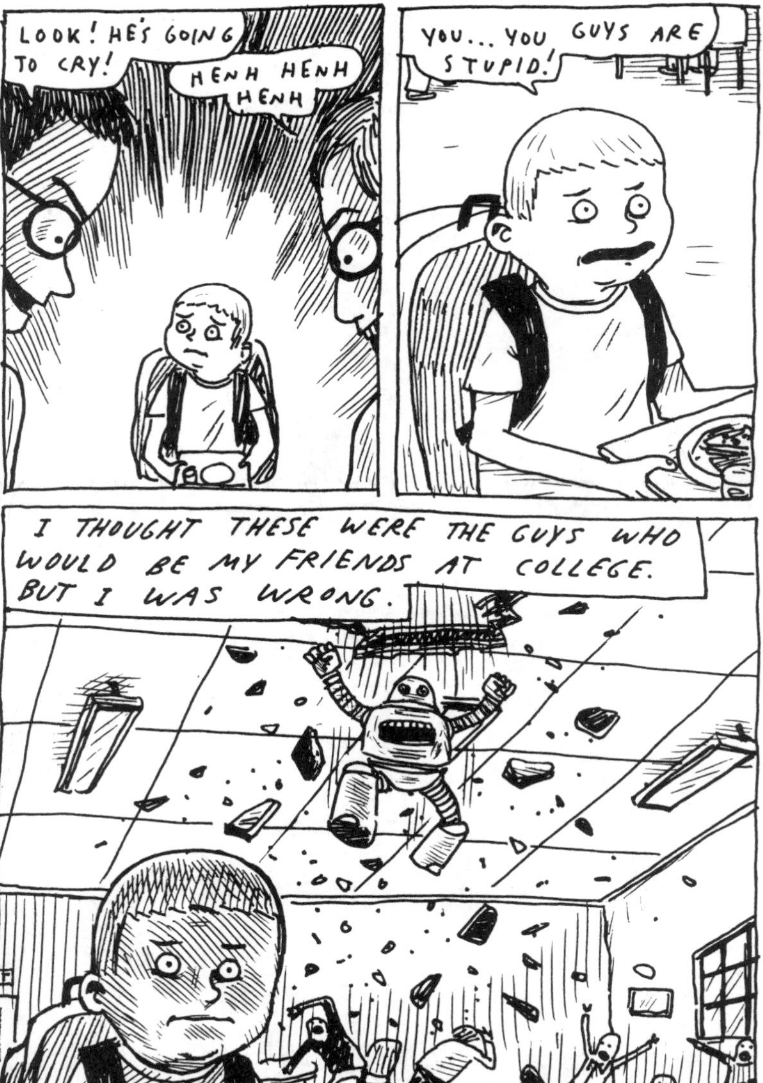
LOOK! HE'S GOING TO CRY!
HENH HENH HENH
YOU... YOU GUYS ARE STUPID!
I THOUGHT THESE WERE THE GUYS WHO WOULD BE MY FRIENDS AT COLLEGE. BUT I WAS WRONG.

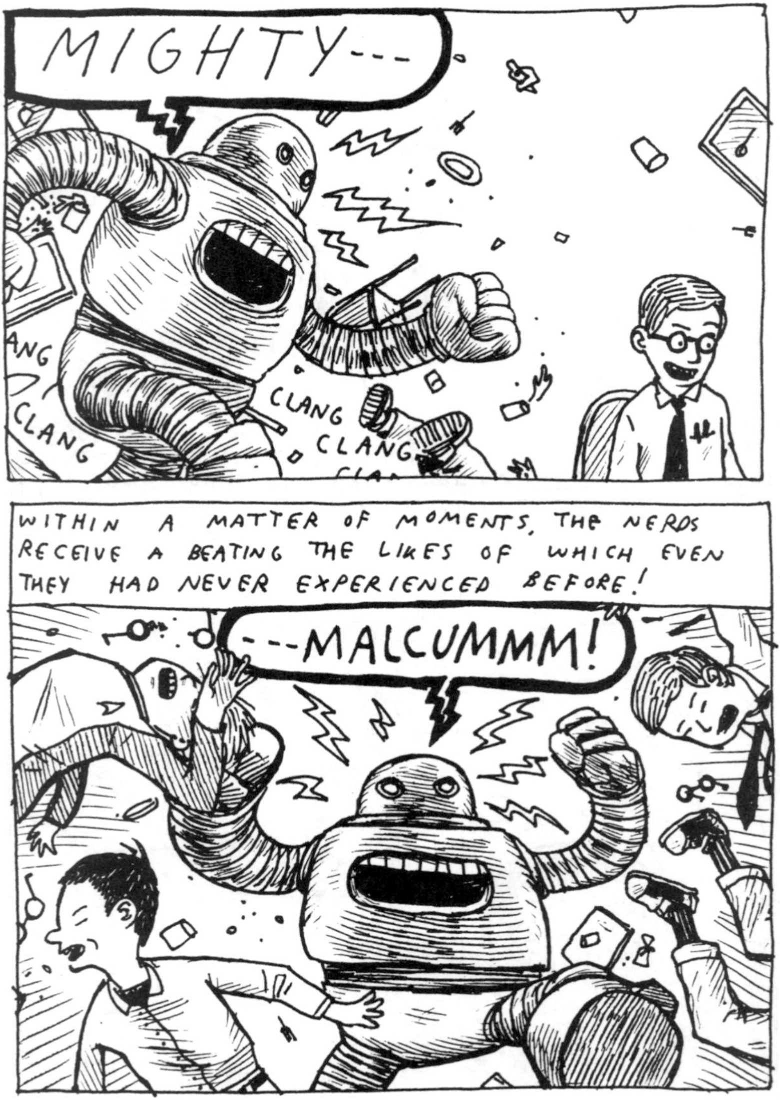
MIGHTY---
ANG
CLANG
CLANG
CLANG
WITHIN A MATTER OF MOMENTS, THE NERDS RECEIVE A BEATING THE LIKES OF WHICH EVEN THEY HAD NEVER EXPERIENCED BEFORE!
---MALCUMMM!

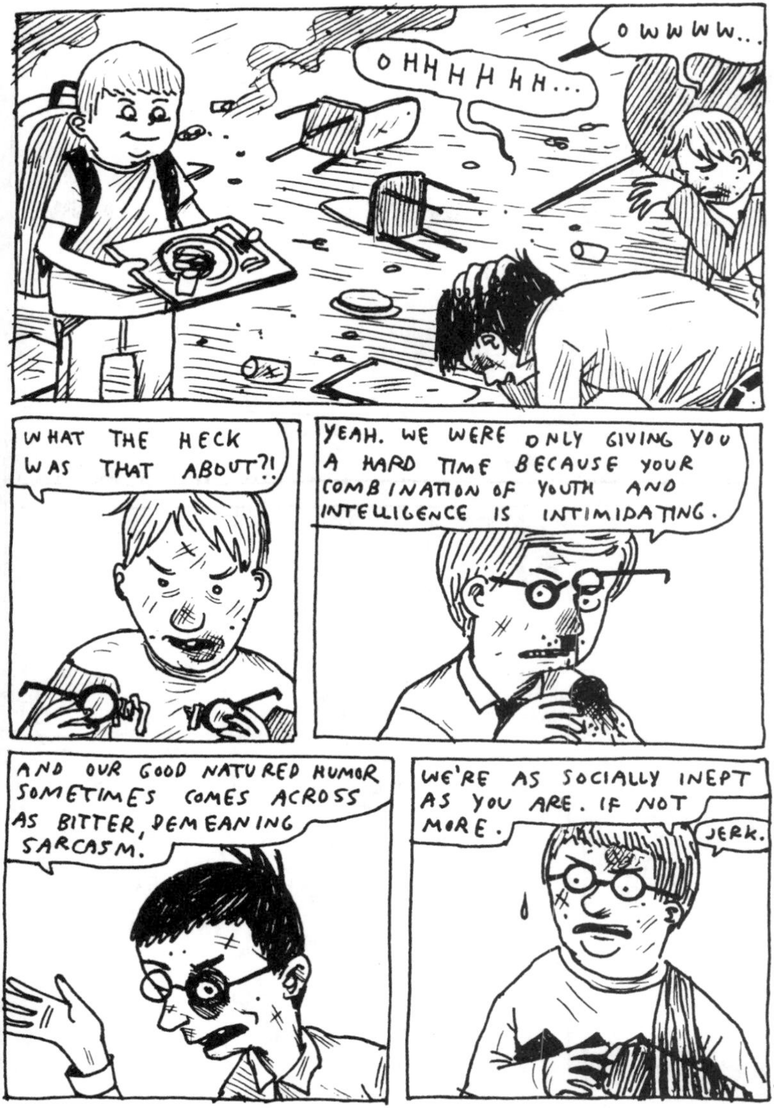
OHHHHHH...
OWWWW...
WHAT THE HECK WAS THAT ABOUT?!
YEAH. WE WERE ONLY GIVING YOU A HARD TIME BECAUSE YOUR COMBINATION OF YOUTH AND INTELLIGENCE IS INTIMIDATING.
AND OUR GOOD NATURED HUMOR SOMETIMES COMES ACROSS AS BITTER, DEMEANING SARCASM.
WE'RE AS SOCIALLY INEPT AS YOU ARE. IF NOT MORE.
JERK.

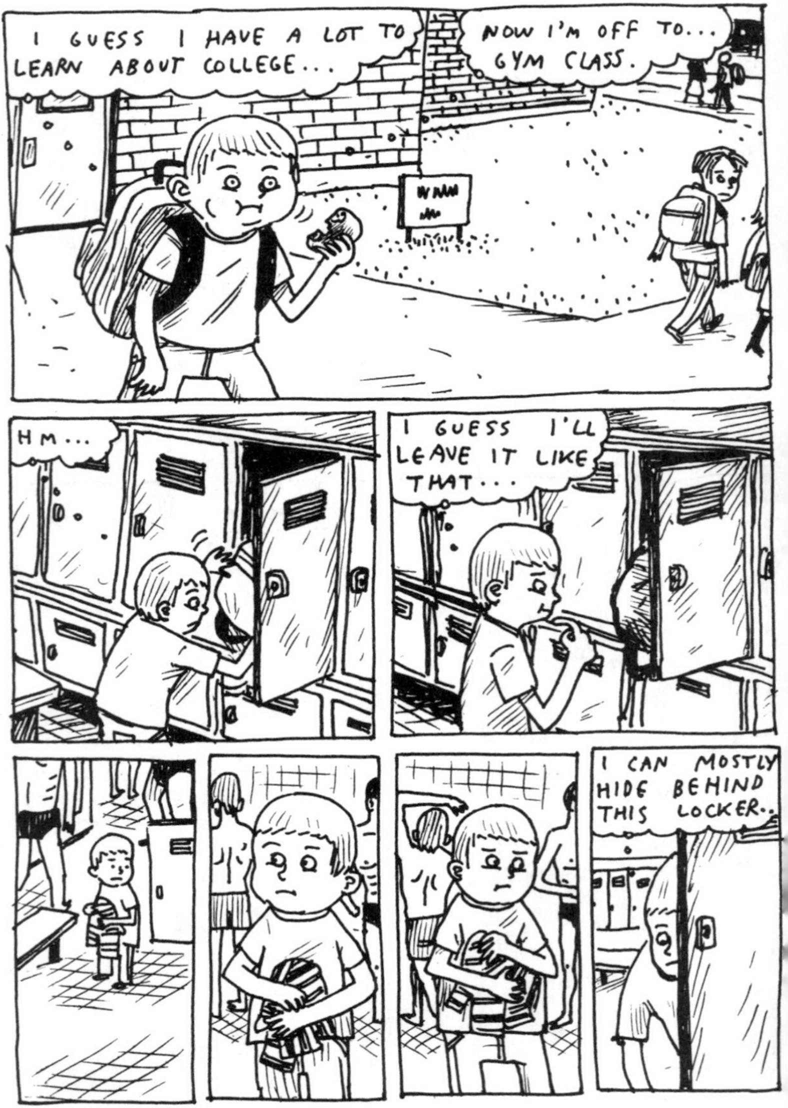
I GUESS I HAVE A LOT TO LEARN ABOUT COLLEGE...
NOW I'M OFF TO... GYM CLASS.
HM...
I GUESS I'LL LEAVE IT LIKE THAT...
I CAN MOSTLY HIDE BEHIND THIS LOCKER..

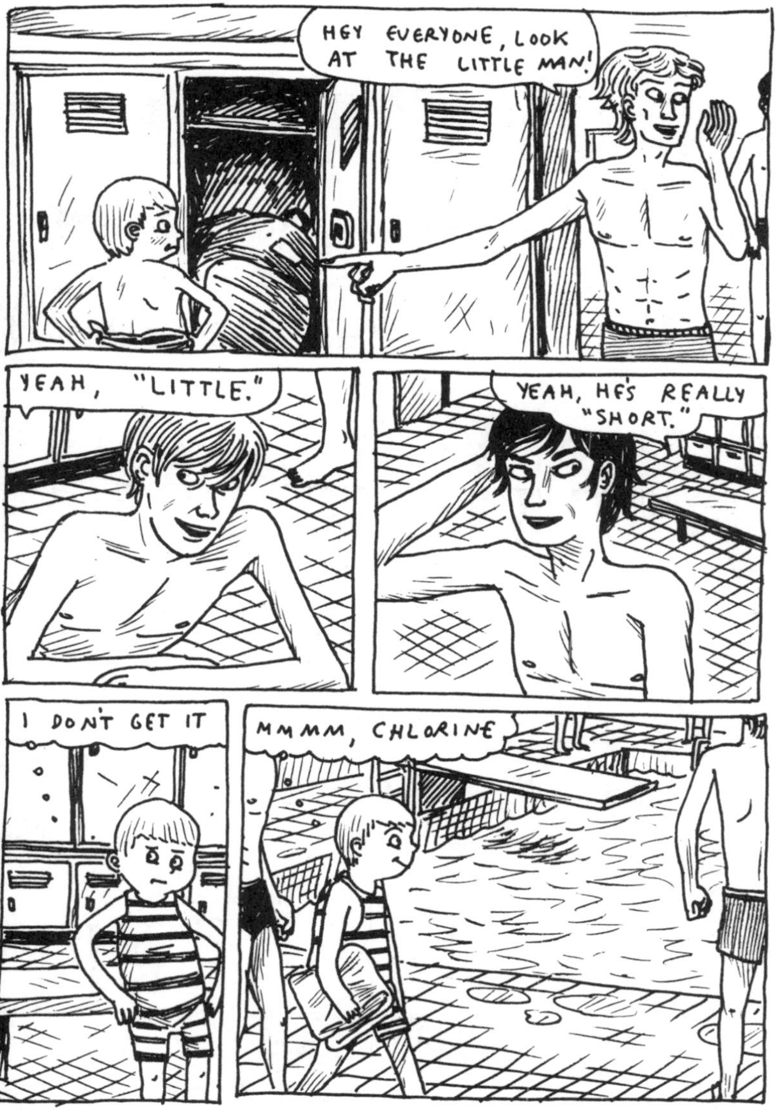
HEY EVERYONE, LOOK AT THE LITTLE MAN!
YEAH, "LITTLE."
YEAH, HE'S REALLY "SHORT."
I DON'T GET IT
MMMM, CHLORINE

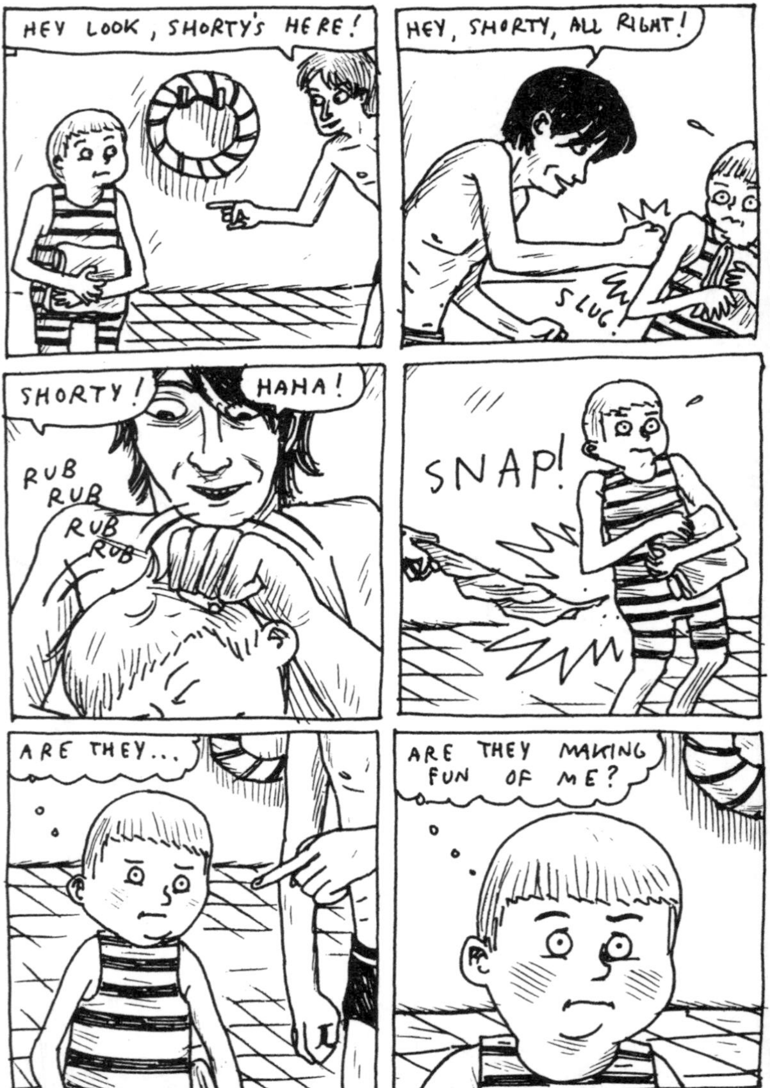
HEY LOOK, SHORTY'S HERE!
HEY, SHORTY, ALL RIGHT!
SLUG!
SHORTY!
HAHA!
RUB RUB RUB RUB
SNAP!
ARE THEY...
ARE THEY MAKING FUN OF ME?

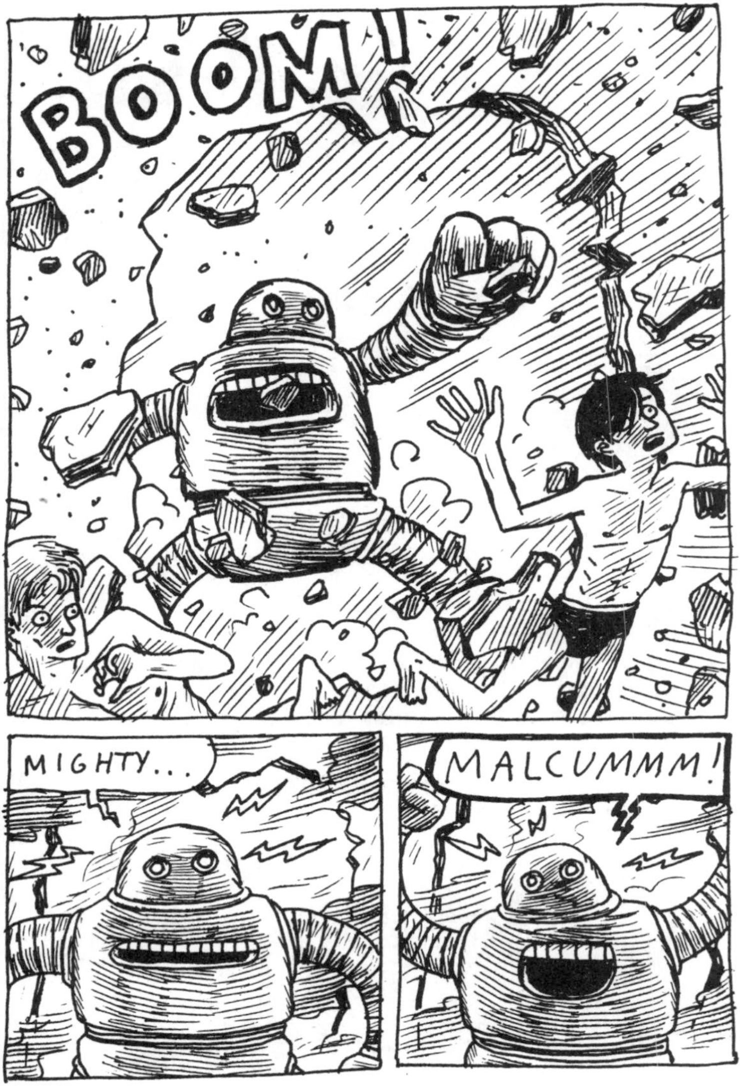
BOOM!
MIGHTY...
MALCUMMM!

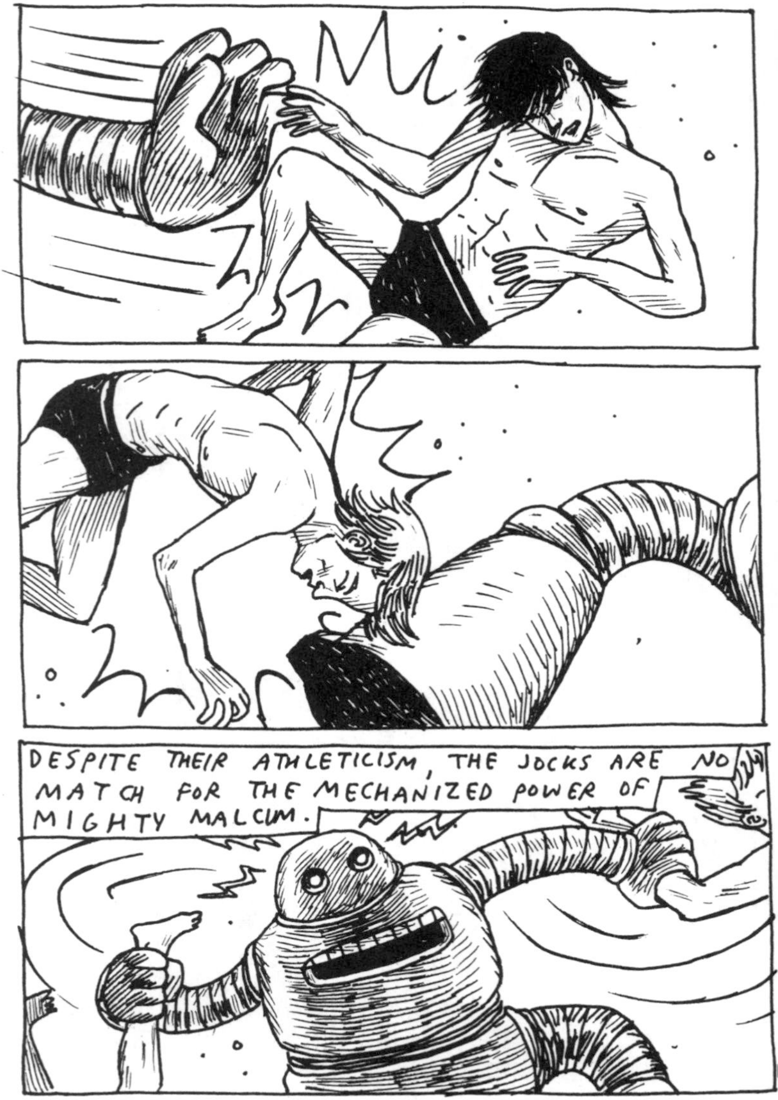
DESPITE THEIR ATHLETICISM, THE JOCKS ARE NO MATCH FOR THE MECHANIZED POWER OF MIGHTY MALCUM.

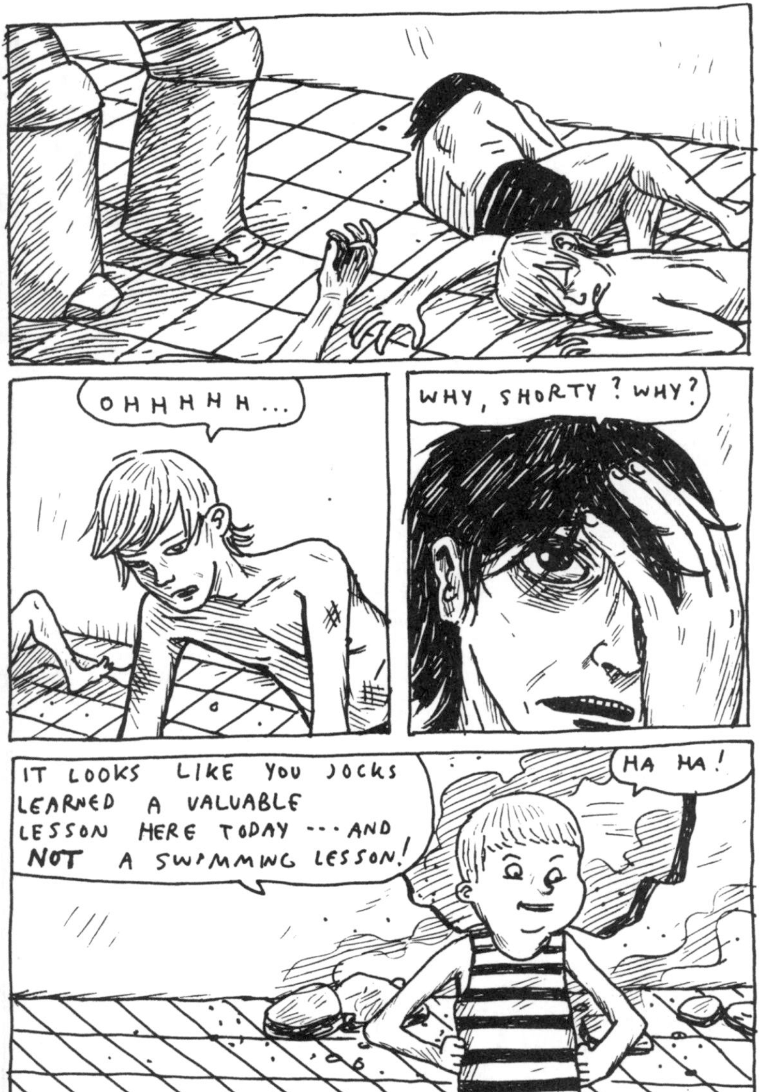
OHHHHH...
WHY, SHORTY? WHY?
IT LOOKS LIKE YOU JOCKS LEARNED A VALUABLE LESSON HERE TODAY --- AND NOT A SWIMMING LESSON!
HA HA!

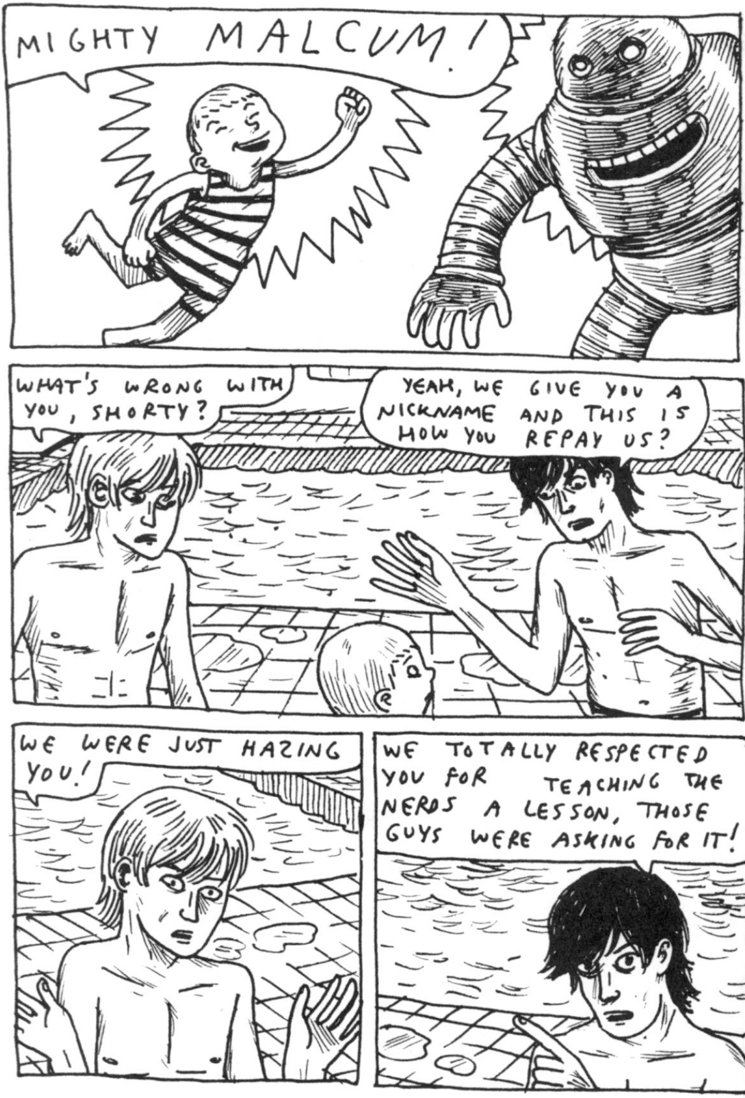
MIGHTY MALCUM!
WHAT'S WRONG WITH YOU, SHORTY?
YEAH, WE GIVE YOU A NICKNAME AND THIS IS HOW YOU REPAY US?
WE WERE JUST HAZING YOU!
WE TOTALLY RESPECTED YOU FOR TEACHING THE NERDS A LESSON, THOSE GUYS WERE ASKING FOR IT!

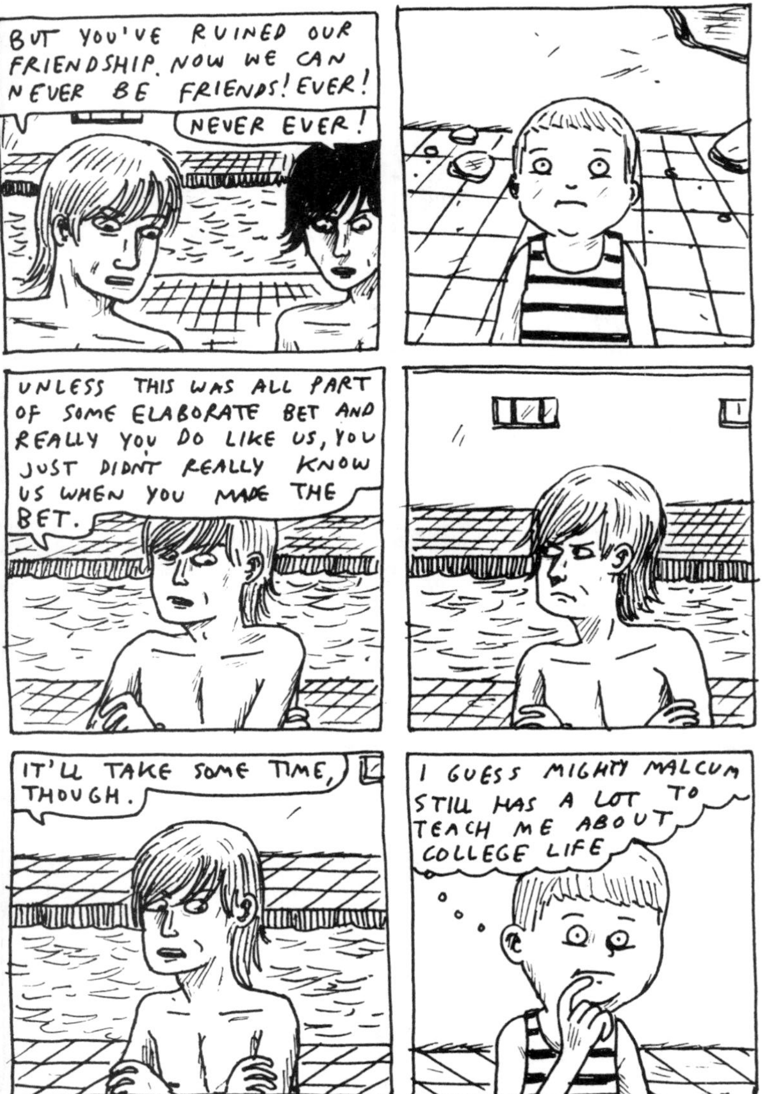
BUT YOU'VE RUINED OUR FRIENDSHIP. NOW WE CAN NEVER BE FRIENDS! EVER!
NEVER EVER!
UNLESS THIS WAS ALL PART OF SOME ELABORATE BET AND REALLY YOU DO LIKE US, YOU JUST DIDN'T REALLY KNOW US WHEN YOU MADE THE BET.
IT'LL TAKE SOME TIME, THOUGH.
I GUESS MIGHTY MALCUM STILL HAS A LOT TO TEACH ME ABOUT COLLEGE LIFE

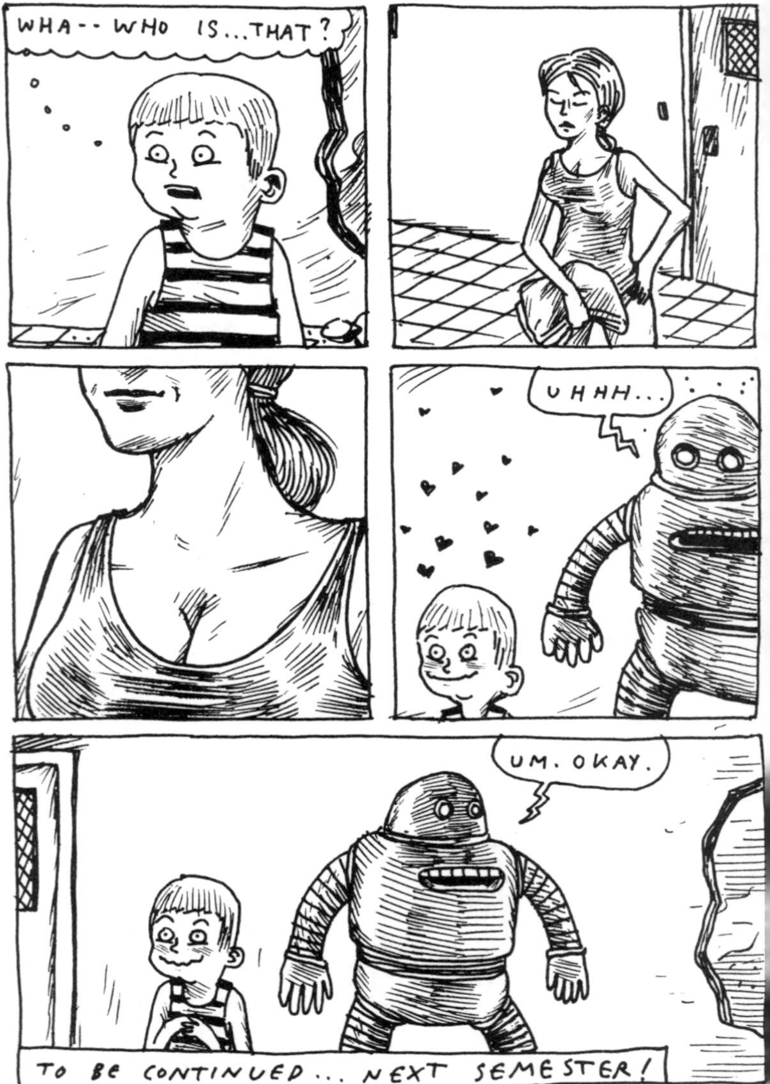

WHA-- WHO IS...THAT?
UHHH...
UM. OKAY.
TO BE CONTINUED... NEXT SEMESTER!

I WILL MAKE LOVE TO YOU

MY BRAND NEW LOVE-MAKING SYSTEM SLAUGHTERS EVERY SINGLE "OLD" MARTIAL ART.

HERE'S THE STORY: AFTER 30 YEARS OF EXPERIENCE OF MAKING OUT IN THE STREET, I SUDDENLY REALIZED THAT EVERY SINGLE PART OF MY BLACK BELT TRAINING HAD GAPING HOLES THAT COULD GET ME KILLED.

SO I SPENT YEARS IN THE STREETS, DEVELOPING A NEW WAY OF LOVEMAKING.

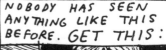

AND I MEAN **NEW**.

NOBODY HAS SEEN ANYTHING LIKE THIS BEFORE. GET THIS:

EVERY MOVE TAKES OUT YOUR LOVER IN ONE SECOND.

THERE ARE NO THROWS, NO LOCKS, NO PUNCHES AND NO KICKS... SO IT'S INCREDIBLY EASY TO LEARN, FAST.

AND, IT IS DESIGNED TO WORK AGAINST LARGER LOVERS.

GROUPS OF THEM, IN FACT.

ACTUALLY, YOU WILL ALMOST WELCOME MULTIPLE LOVERS. THIS IS PROVEN STUFF.

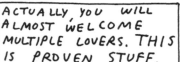

I TRAIN AGAINST MULTIPLE LOVERS ONLY, AND ONLY AGAINST LOVERS WHO OUTWEIGH ME BY TWENTY POUNDS OF MUSCLE.

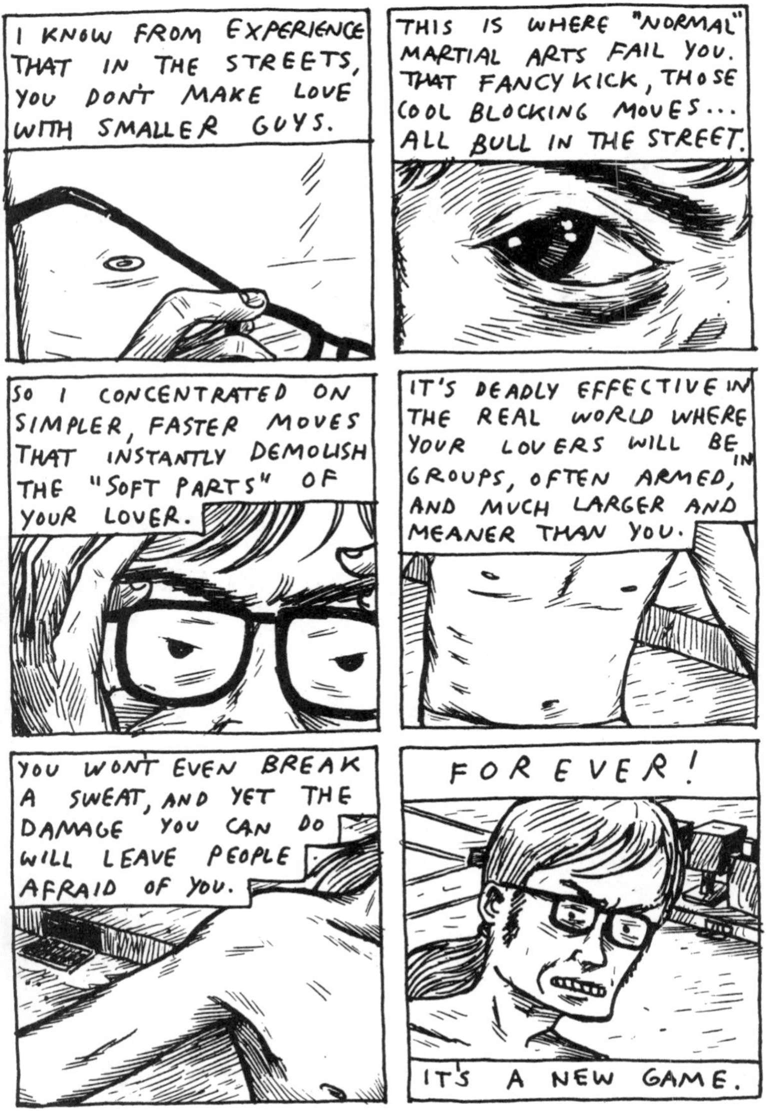
I KNOW FROM EXPERIENCE THAT IN THE STREETS, YOU DON'T MAKE LOVE WITH SMALLER GUYS.
THIS IS WHERE "NORMAL" MARTIAL ARTS FAIL YOU. THAT FANCY KICK, THOSE COOL BLOCKING MOVES... ALL BULL IN THE STREET.
SO I CONCENTRATED ON SIMPLER, FASTER MOVES THAT INSTANTLY DEMOLISH THE "SOFT PARTS" OF YOUR LOVER.
IT'S DEADLY EFFECTIVE IN THE REAL WORLD WHERE YOUR LOVERS WILL BE IN GROUPS, OFTEN ARMED, AND MUCH LARGER AND MEANER THAN YOU.
YOU WON'T EVEN BREAK A SWEAT, AND YET THE DAMAGE YOU CAN DO WILL LEAVE PEOPLE AFRAID OF YOU.
FOREVER!
IT'S A NEW GAME.

IF YOU'RE STILL TRYING TO MAKE LOVE WITH FANCY KICKS AND STRIKES THAT TAKE MORE THAN A SECOND TO COMPLETE... YOU'RE MEAT ON THE STREET.

THIS WILL CHANGE EVERYTHING FOR YOU.

LET THE CREEPS THINK THEY HAVE AN ADVANTAGE OVER YOU, BECAUSE THEY'RE BIGGER, MEANER, OR HAVE A WEAPON.

LET 'EM LAUGH.

THEY ARE JUST SECONDS AWAY FROM SUFFERING SUCH INTENSE LOVE MAKING THAT THEY WILL REMEMBER YOU WITH FEAR FOR THE REST OF THEIR SORRY LIVES!

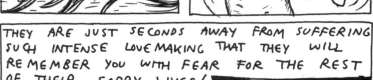

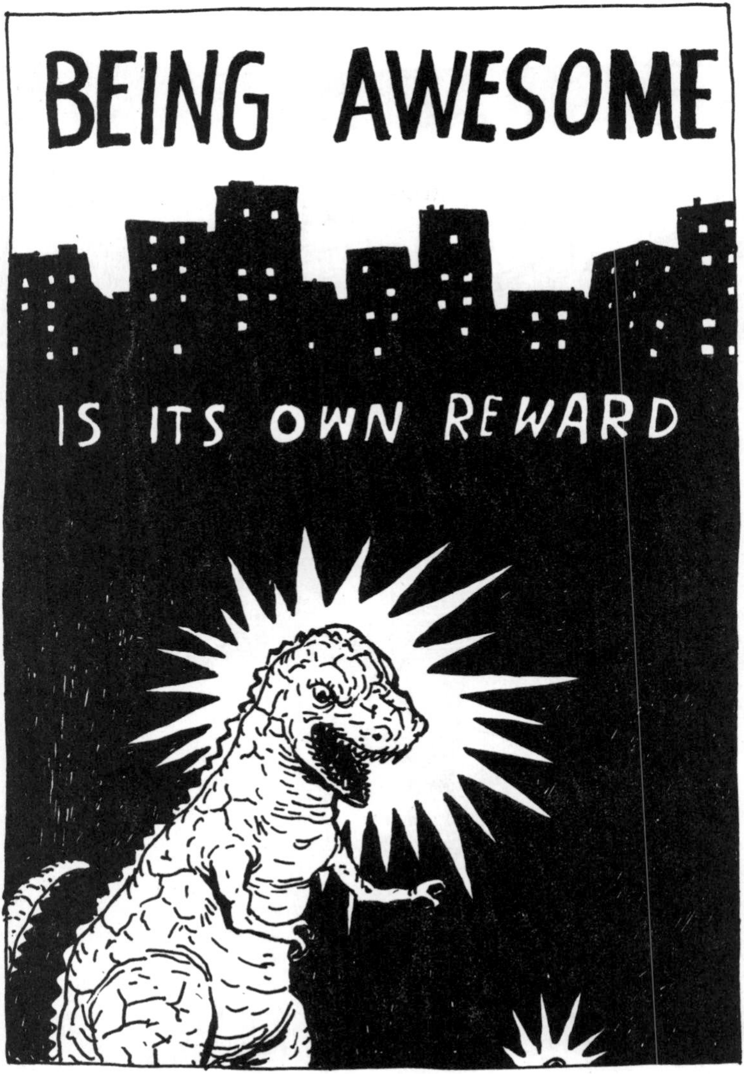
BEING AWESOME
IS ITS OWN REWARD

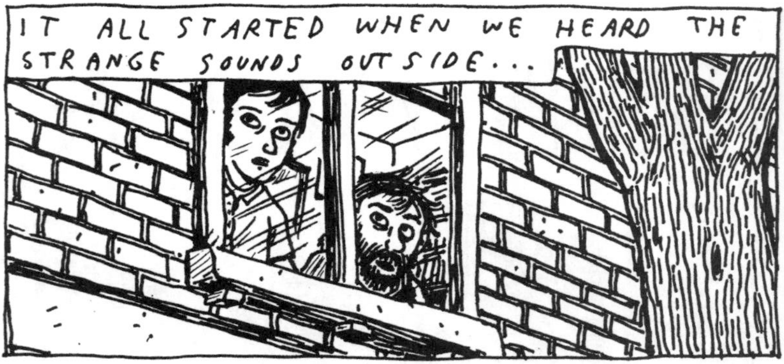
IT ALL STARTED WHEN WE HEARD THE STRANGE SOUNDS OUTSIDE...

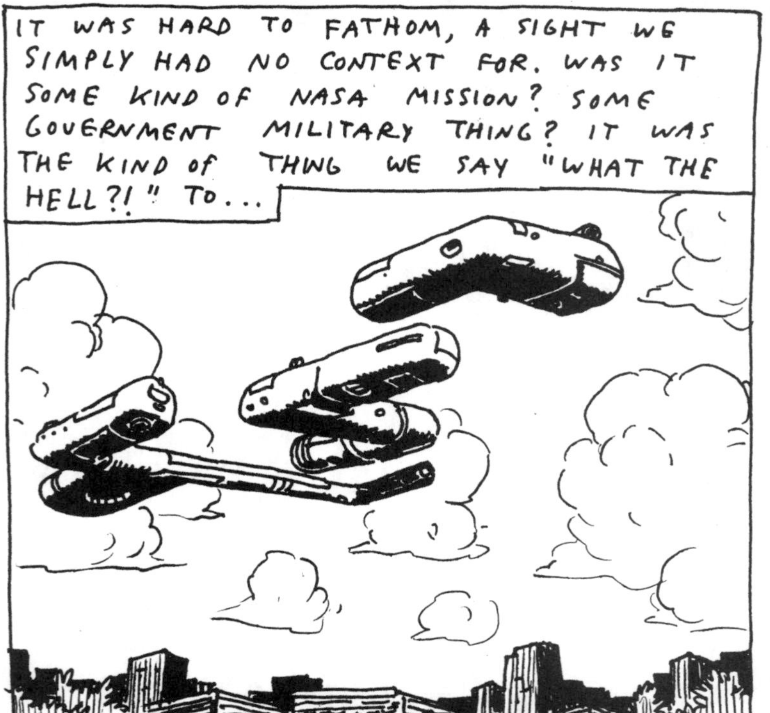
IT WAS HARD TO FATHOM, A SIGHT WE SIMPLY HAD NO CONTEXT FOR. WAS IT SOME KIND OF NASA MISSION? SOME GOVERNMENT MILITARY THING? IT WAS THE KIND OF THING WE SAY "WHAT THE HELL?!" TO...

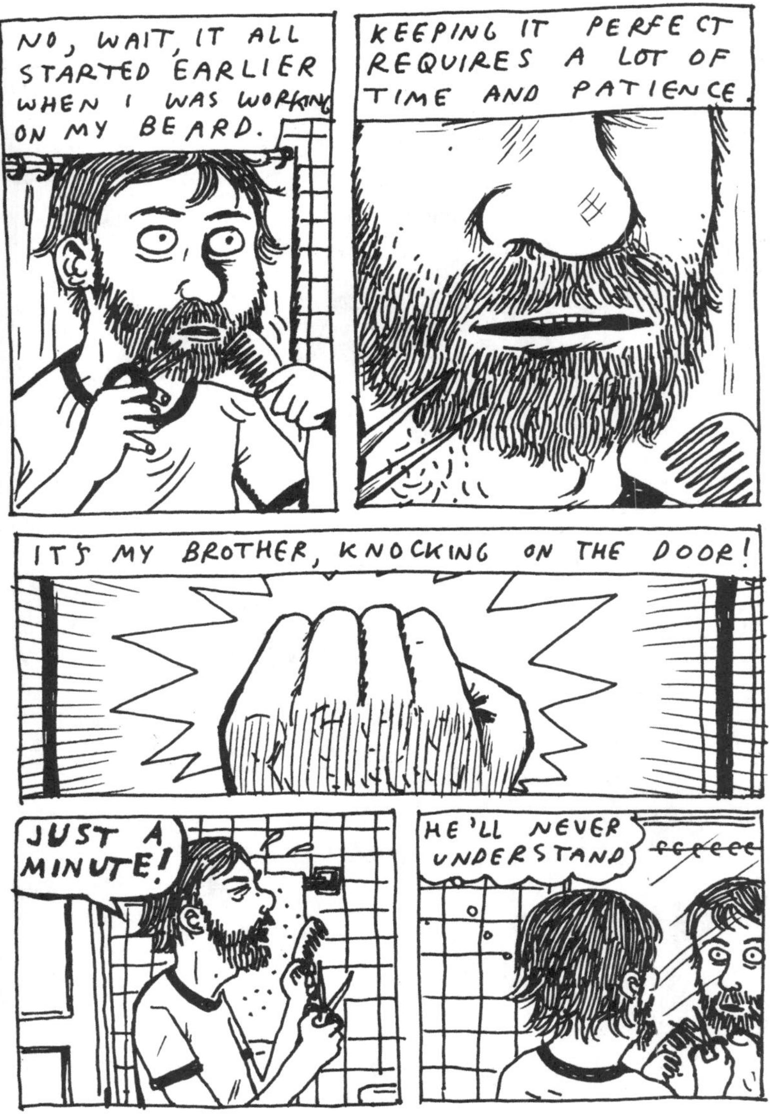
NO, WAIT, IT ALL STARTED EARLIER WHEN I WAS WORKING ON MY BEARD.
KEEPING IT PERFECT REQUIRES A LOT OF TIME AND PATIENCE.
IT'S MY BROTHER, KNOCKING ON THE DOOR!
JUST A MINUTE!
HE'LL NEVER UNDERSTAND

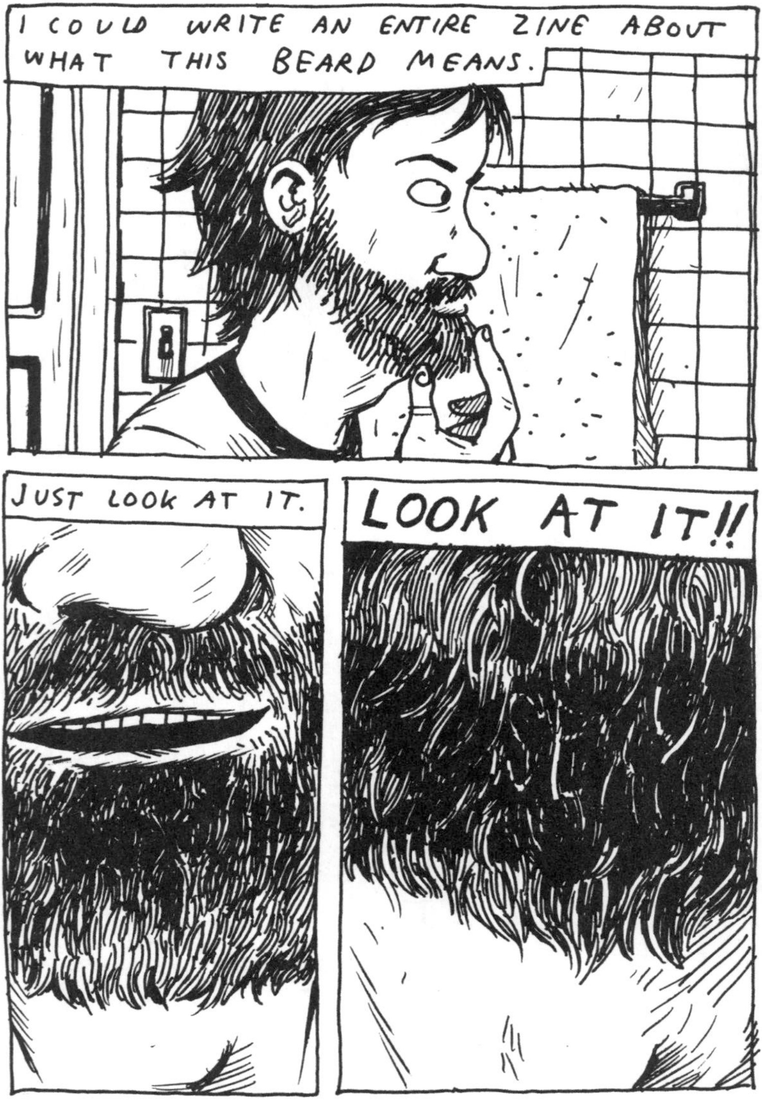
I COULD WRITE AN ENTIRE ZINE ABOUT WHAT THIS BEARD MEANS.
JUST LOOK AT IT.
LOOK AT IT!!

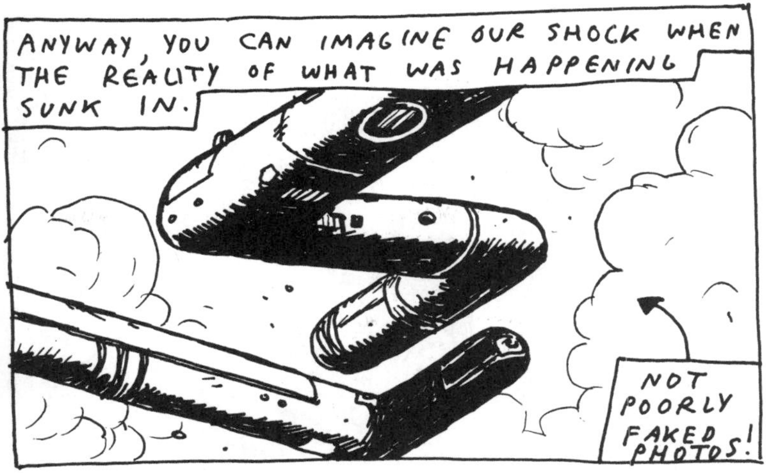
ANYWAY, YOU CAN IMAGINE OUR SHOCK WHEN THE REALITY OF WHAT WAS HAPPENING SUNK IN.
NOT POORLY FAKED PHOTOS!

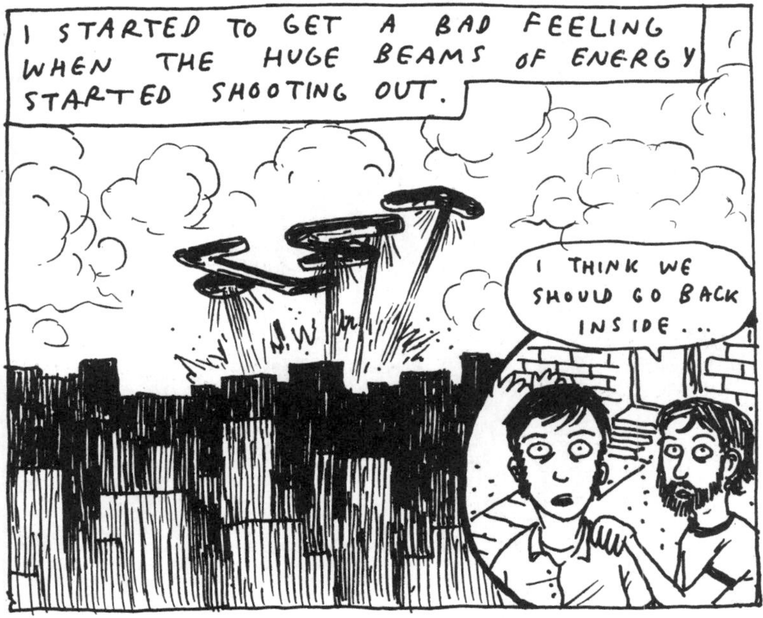
I STARTED TO GET A BAD FEELING WHEN THE HUGE BEAMS OF ENERGY STARTED SHOOTING OUT.
I THINK WE SHOULD GO BACK INSIDE...

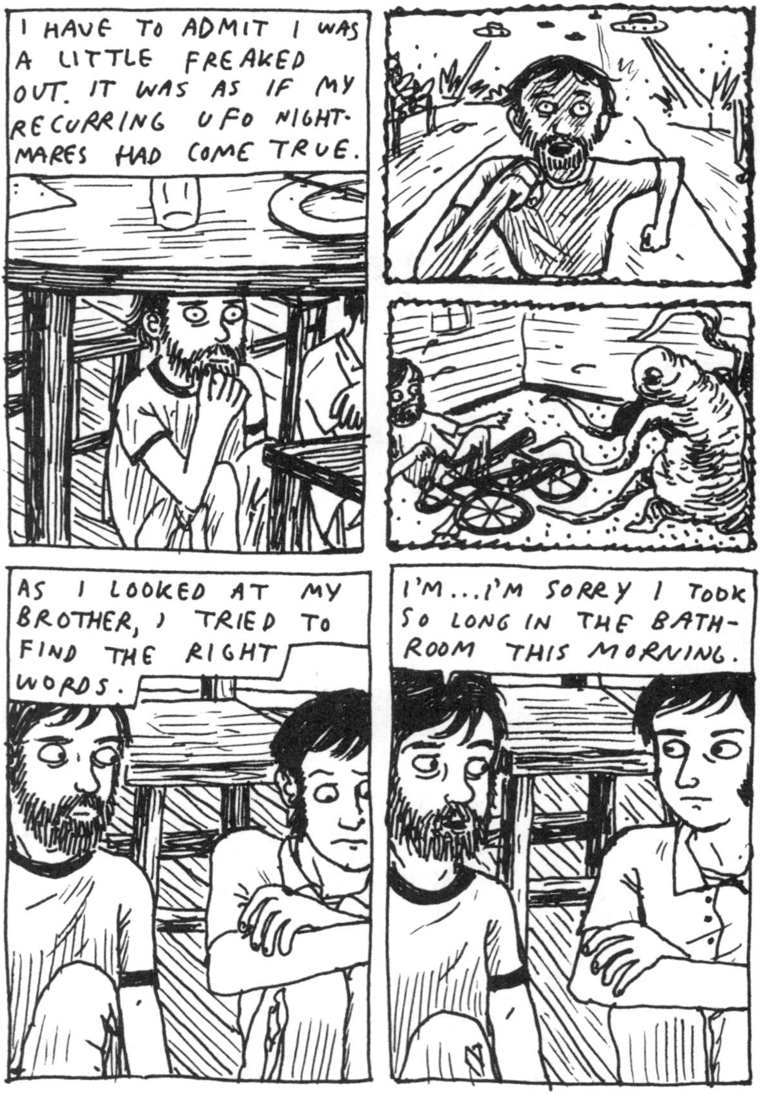
I HAVE TO ADMIT I WAS A LITTLE FREAKED OUT. IT WAS AS IF MY RECURRING UFO NIGHT-MARES HAD COME TRUE.
AS I LOOKED AT MY BROTHER, I TRIED TO FIND THE RIGHT WORDS.
I'M...I'M SORRY I TOOK SO LONG IN THE BATH-ROOM THIS MORNING.

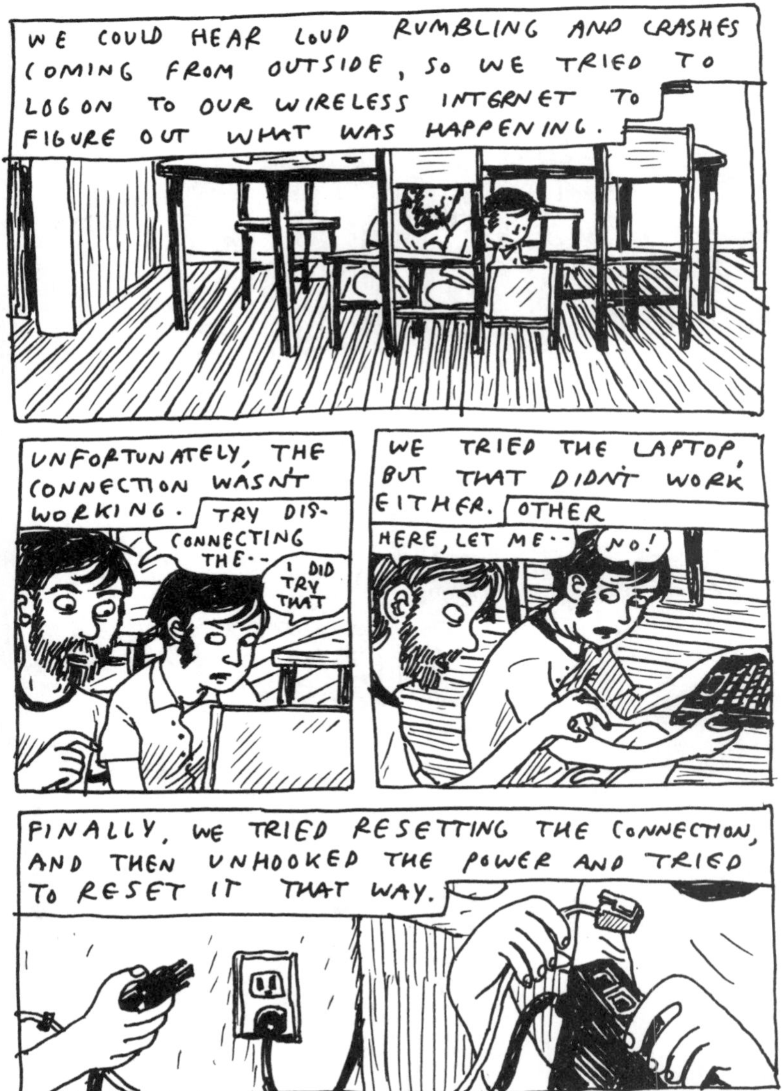
WE COULD HEAR LOUD RUMBLING AND CRASHES COMING FROM OUTSIDE, SO WE TRIED TO LOG ON TO OUR WIRELESS INTERNET TO FIGURE OUT WHAT WAS HAPPENING.
UNFORTUNATELY, THE CONNECTION WASN'T WORKING.
TRY DIS-CONNECTING THE--
I DID TRY THAT
WE TRIED THE LAPTOP, BUT THAT DIDN'T WORK EITHER.
OTHER
HERE, LET ME--
NO!
FINALLY, WE TRIED RESETTING THE CONNECTION, AND THEN UNHOOKED THE POWER AND TRIED TO RESET IT THAT WAY.

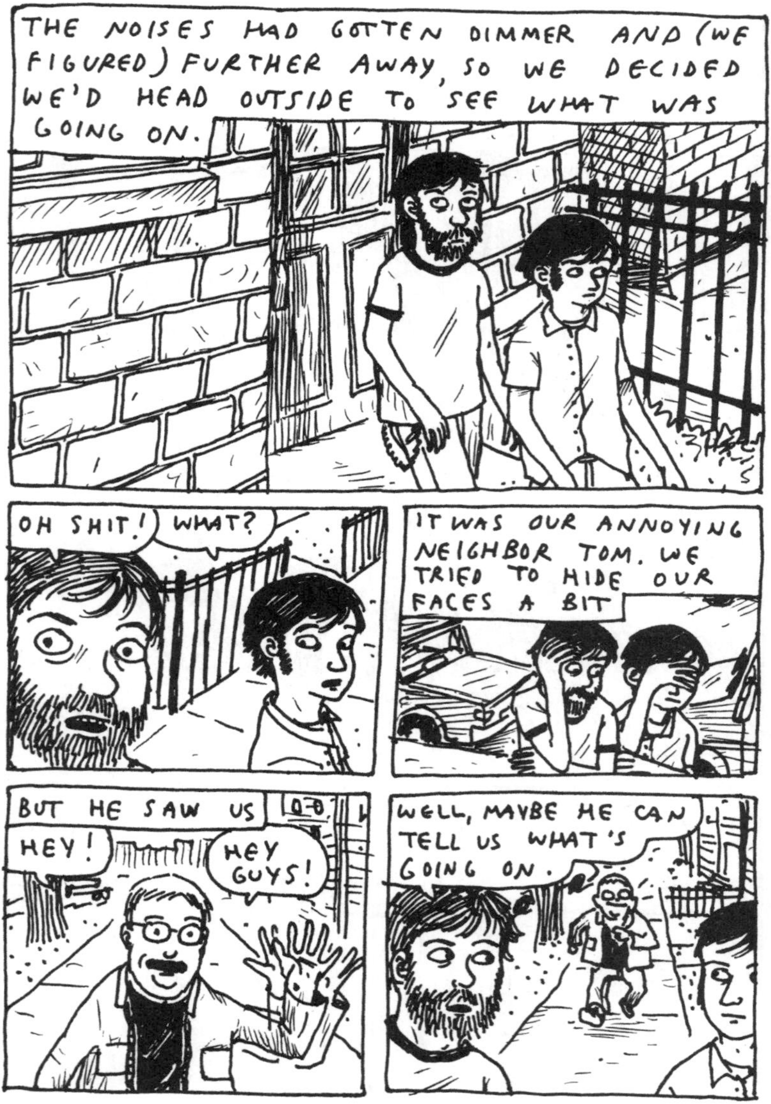
THE NOISES HAD GOTTEN DIMMER AND (WE FIGURED) FURTHER AWAY, SO WE DECIDED WE'D HEAD OUTSIDE TO SEE WHAT WAS GOING ON.
OH SHIT!
WHAT?
IT WAS OUR ANNOYING NEIGHBOR TOM. WE TRIED TO HIDE OUR FACES A BIT
BUT HE SAW US
HEY!
HEY GUYS!
WELL, MAYBE HE CAN TELL US WHAT'S GOING ON.

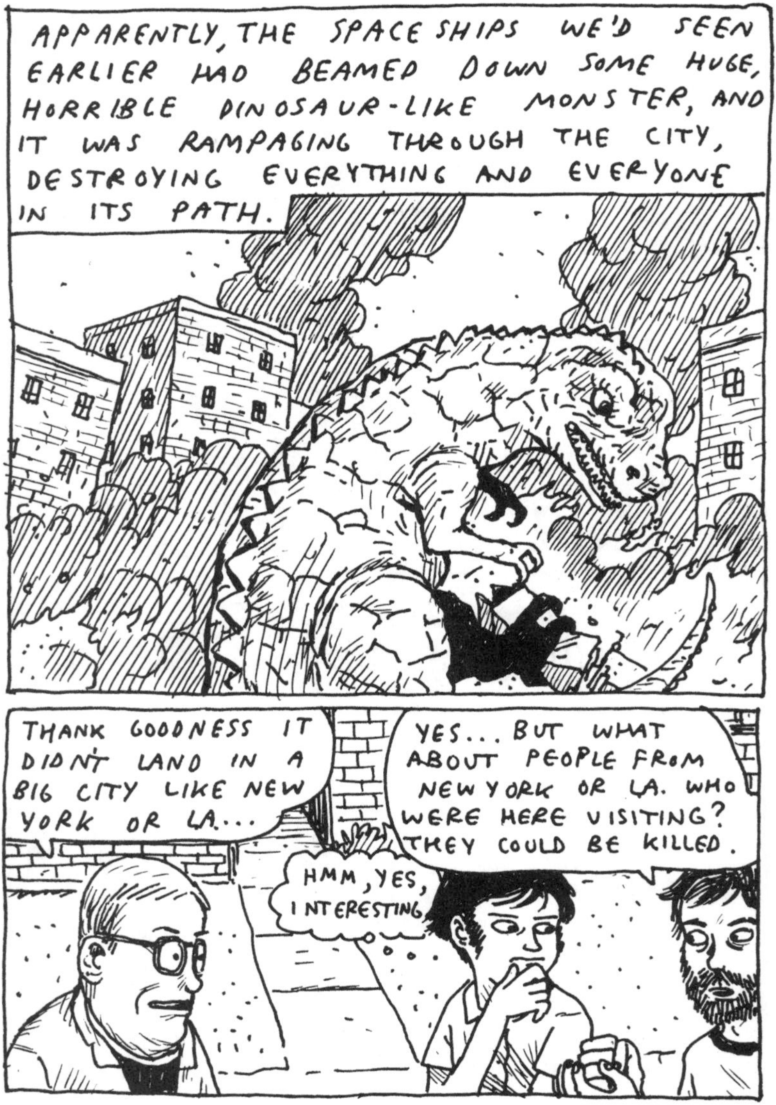
APPARENTLY, THE SPACE SHIPS WE'D SEEN EARLIER HAD BEAMED DOWN SOME HUGE, HORRIBLE DINOSAUR-LIKE MONSTER, AND IT WAS RAMPAGING THROUGH THE CITY, DESTROYING EVERYTHING AND EVERYONE IN ITS PATH.
THANK GOODNESS IT DIDN'T LAND IN A BIG CITY LIKE NEW YORK OR LA...
YES... BUT WHAT ABOUT PEOPLE FROM NEW YORK OR LA. WHO WERE HERE VISITING? THEY COULD BE KILLED.
HMM, YES, INTERESTING

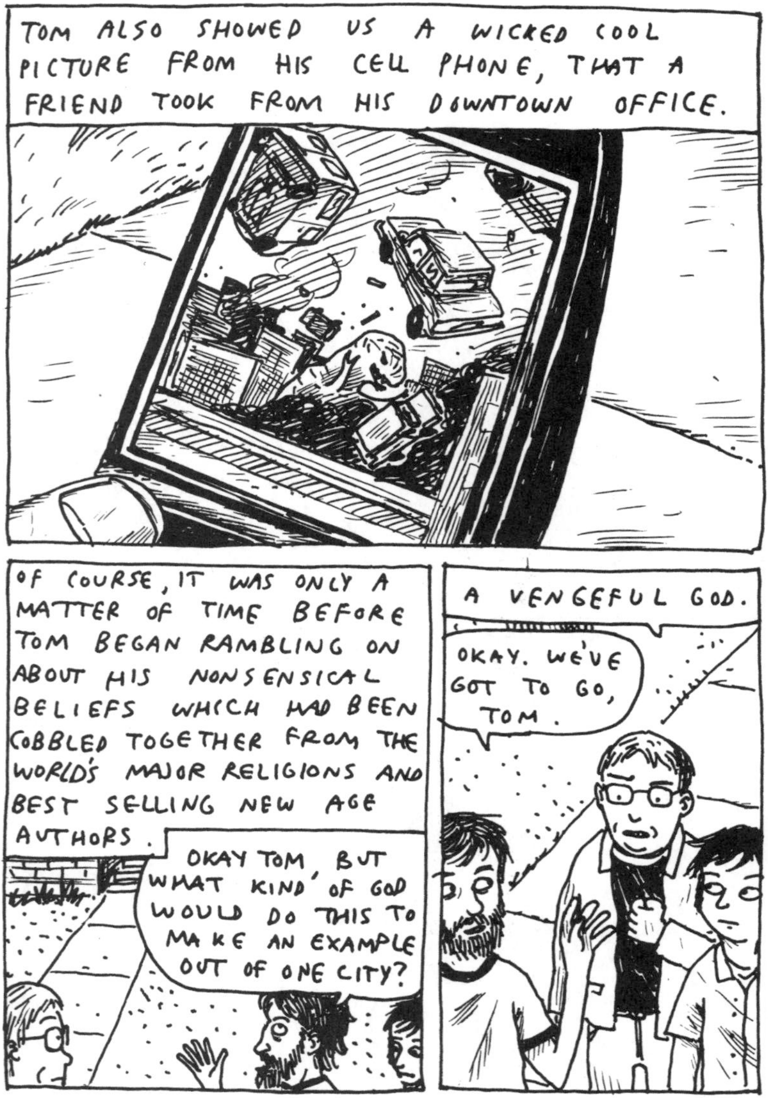
TOM ALSO SHOWED US A WICKED COOL PICTURE FROM HIS CELL PHONE, THAT A FRIEND TOOK FROM HIS DOWNTOWN OFFICE.
OF COURSE, IT WAS ONLY A MATTER OF TIME BEFORE TOM BEGAN RAMBLING ON ABOUT HIS NONSENSICAL BELIEFS WHICH HAD BEEN COBBLED TOGETHER FROM THE WORLD'S MAJOR RELIGIONS AND BEST SELLING NEW AGE AUTHORS.
OKAY TOM, BUT WHAT KIND OF GOD WOULD DO THIS TO MAKE AN EXAMPLE OUT OF ONE CITY?
A VENGEFUL GOD.
OKAY. WE'VE GOT TO GO, TOM.

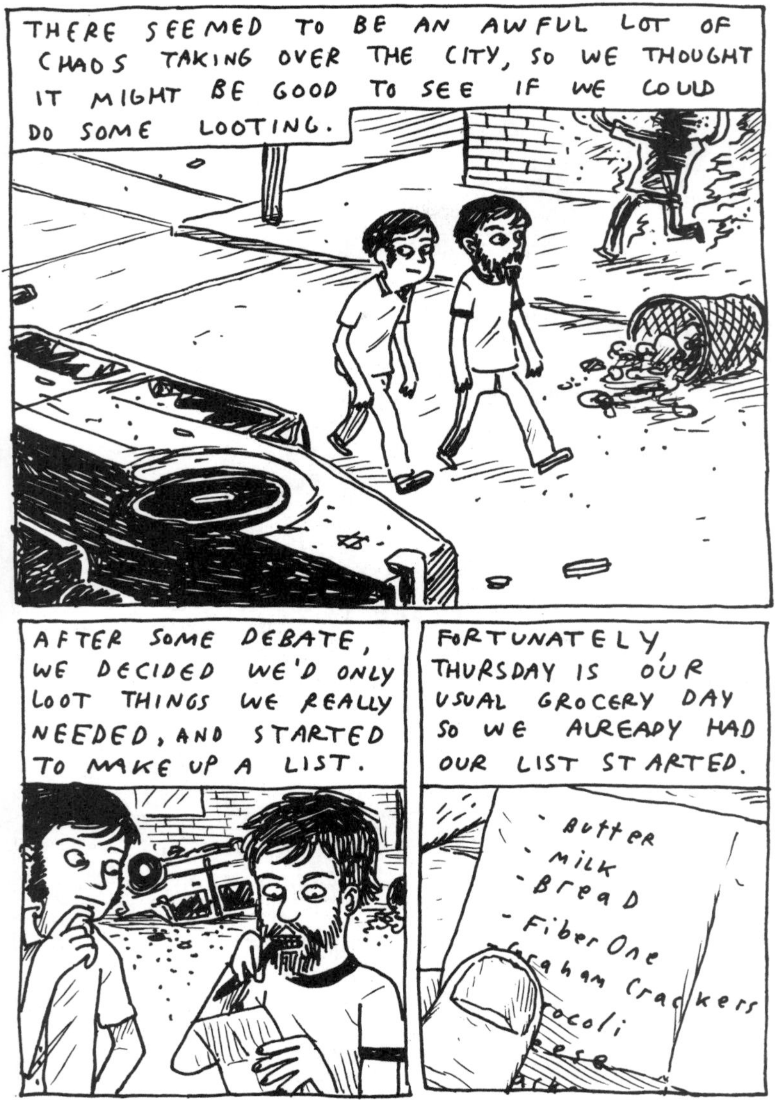
THERE SEEMED TO BE AN AWFUL LOT OF CHAOS TAKING OVER THE CITY, SO WE THOUGHT IT MIGHT BE GOOD TO SEE IF WE COULD DO SOME LOOTING.
AFTER SOME DEBATE, WE DECIDED WE'D ONLY LOOT THINGS WE REALLY NEEDED, AND STARTED TO MAKE UP A LIST.
FORTUNATELY, THURSDAY IS OUR USUAL GROCERY DAY SO WE ALREADY HAD OUR LIST STARTED.
- Butter
- milk
- Bread
- Fiber One

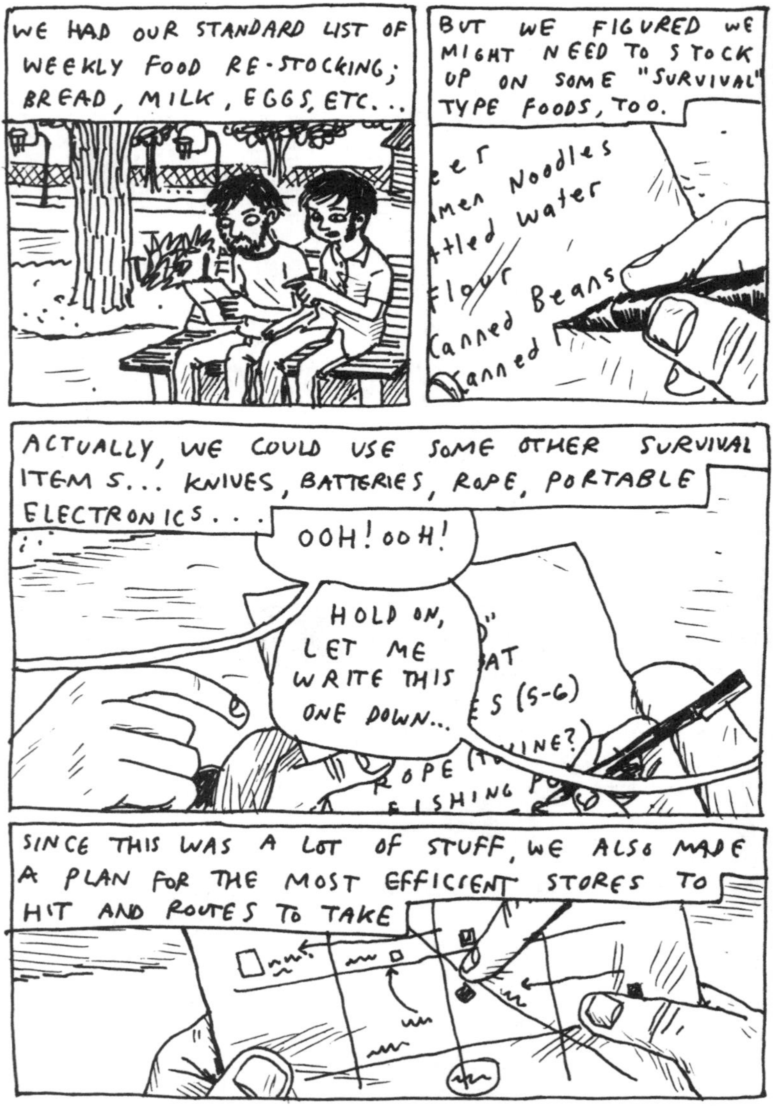
WE HAD OUR STANDARD LIST OF WEEKLY FOOD RE-STOCKING; BREAD, MILK, EGGS, ETC...
BUT WE FIGURED WE MIGHT NEED TO STOCK UP ON SOME "SURVIVAL" TYPE FOODS, TOO.
Noodles
water
Flour
Canned Beans
Canned
ACTUALLY, WE COULD USE SOME OTHER SURVIVAL ITEMS... KNIVES, BATTERIES, ROPE, PORTABLE ELECTRONICS...
OOH! OOH!
HOLD ON, LET ME WRITE THIS ONE DOWN...
ROPE
FISHING
SINCE THIS WAS A LOT OF STUFF, WE ALSO MADE A PLAN FOR THE MOST EFFICIENT STORES TO HIT AND ROUTES TO TAKE

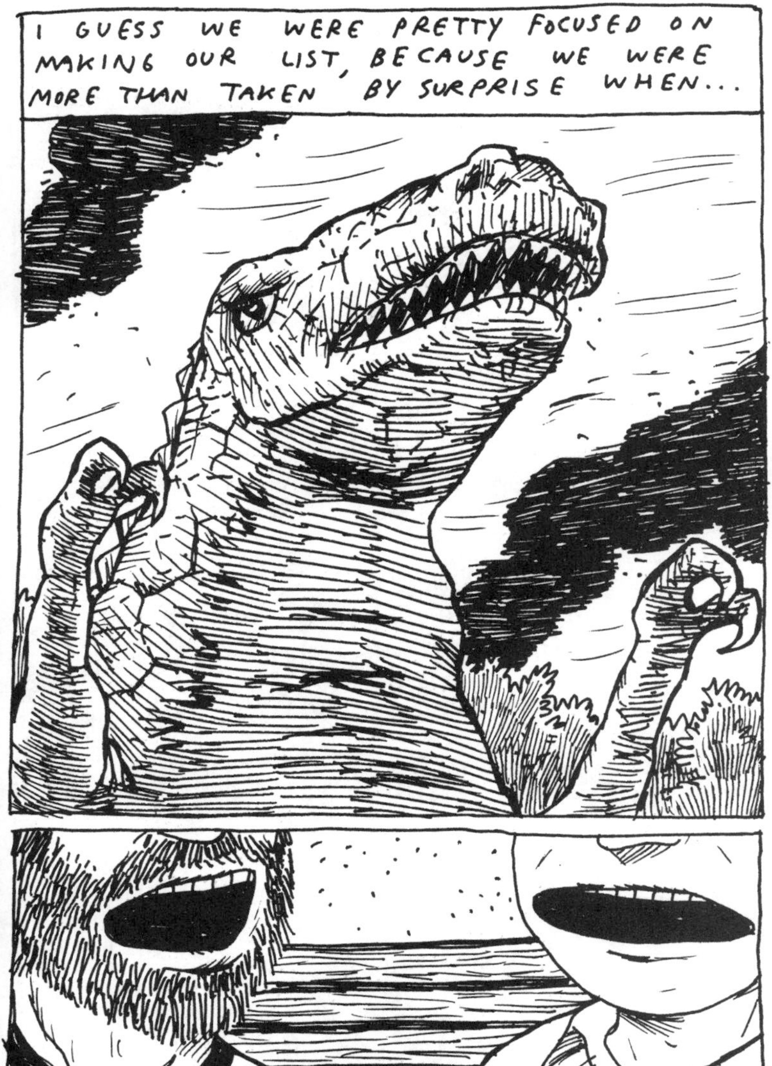
I GUESS WE WERE PRETTY FOCUSED ON MAKING OUR LIST, BECAUSE WE WERE MORE THAN TAKEN BY SURPRISE WHEN...

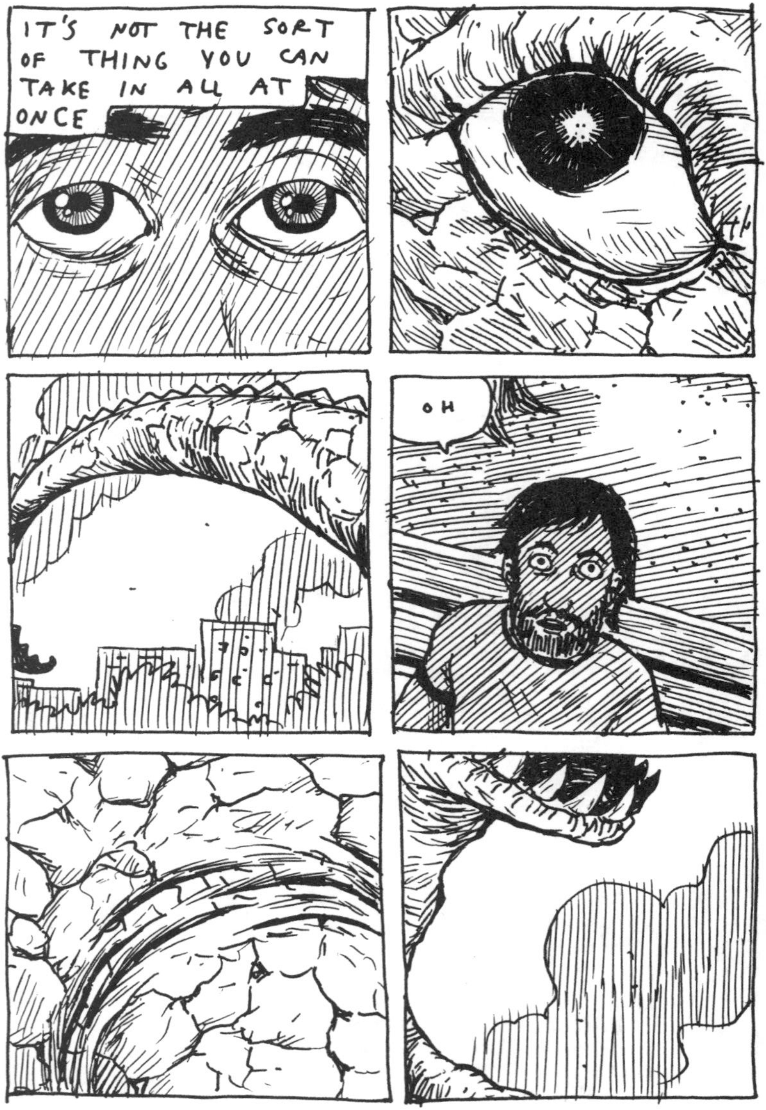
IT'S NOT THE SORT OF THING YOU CAN TAKE IN ALL AT ONCE
OH

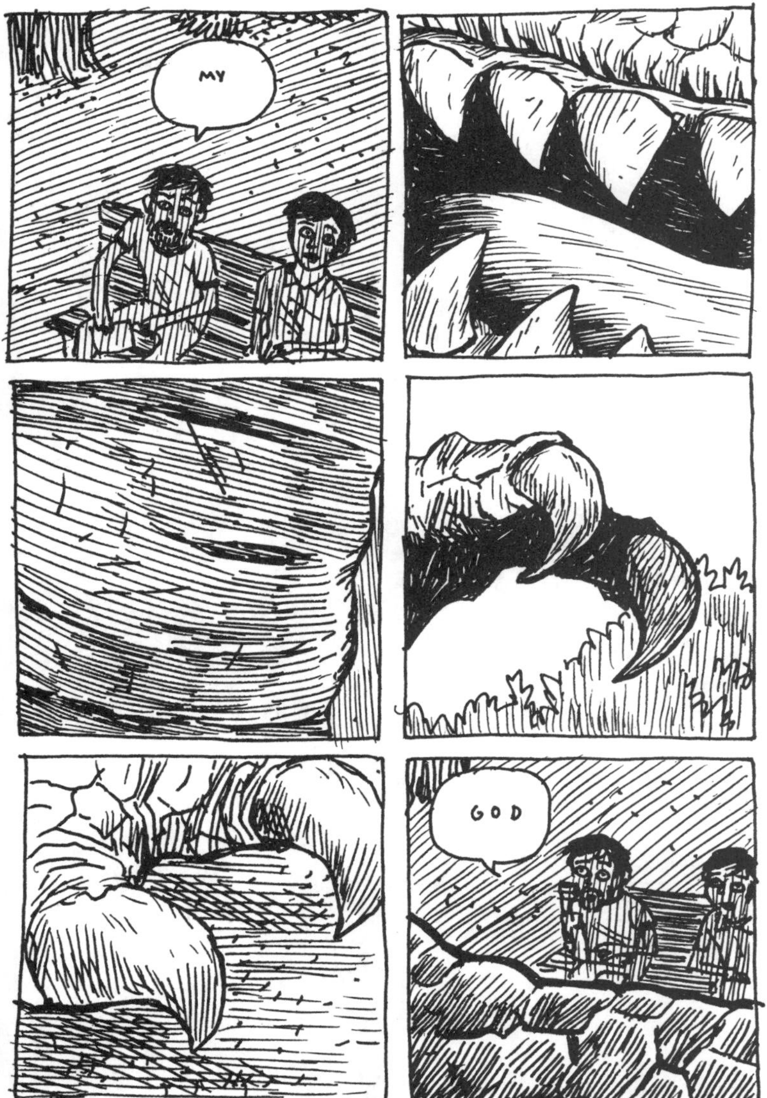
MY
GOD

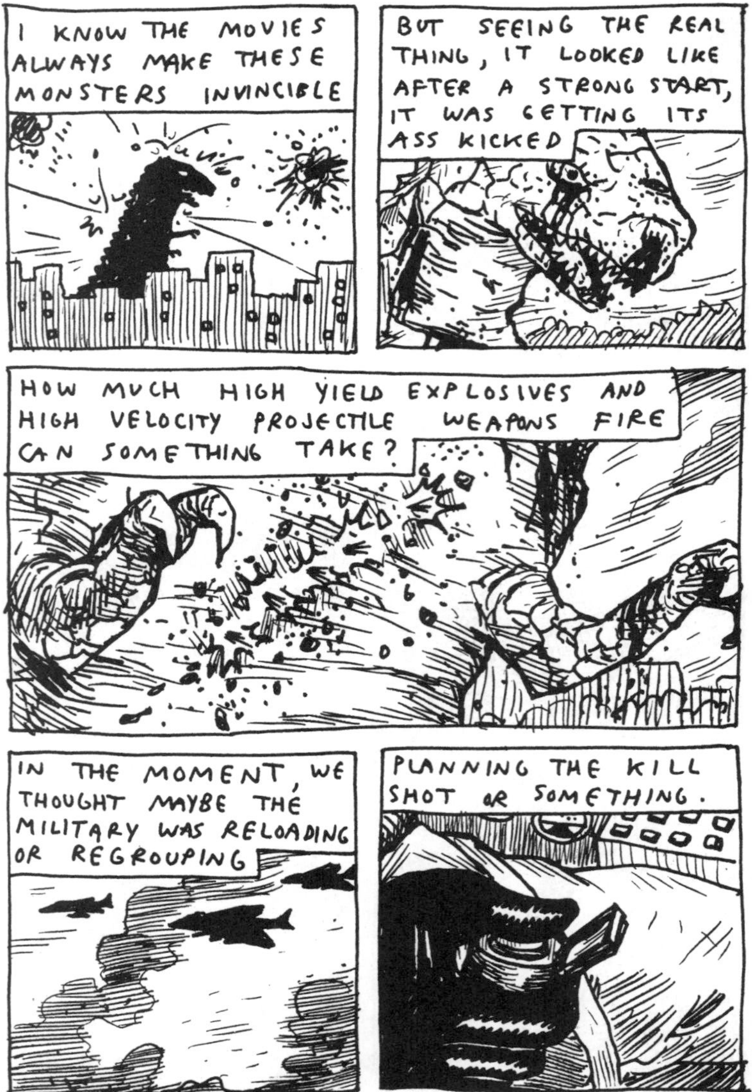
I KNOW THE MOVIES ALWAYS MAKE THESE MONSTERS INVINCIBLE
BUT SEEING THE REAL THING, IT LOOKED LIKE AFTER A STRONG START, IT WAS GETTING ITS ASS KICKED
HOW MUCH HIGH YIELD EXPLOSIVES AND HIGH VELOCITY PROJECTILE WEAPONS FIRE CAN SOMETHING TAKE?
IN THE MOMENT, WE THOUGHT MAYBE THE MILITARY WAS RELOADING OR REGROUPING
PLANNING THE KILL SHOT OR SOMETHING.

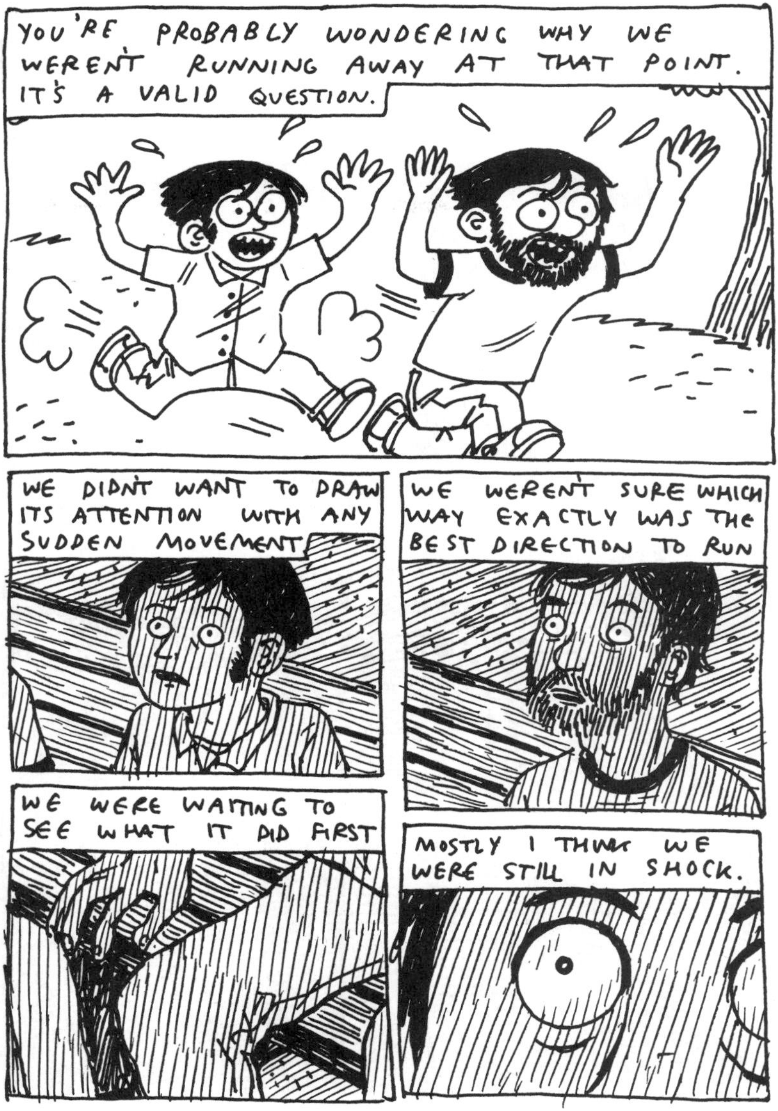
YOU'RE PROBABLY WONDERING WHY WE WERENT RUNNING AWAY AT THAT POINT. IT'S A VALID QUESTION.
WE DIDN'T WANT TO DRAW ITS ATTENTION WITH ANY SUDDEN MOVEMENT
WE WERENT SURE WHICH WAY EXACTLY WAS THE BEST DIRECTION TO RUN
WE WERE WAITING TO SEE WHAT IT DID FIRST
MOSTLY I THINK WE WERE STILL IN SHOCK.

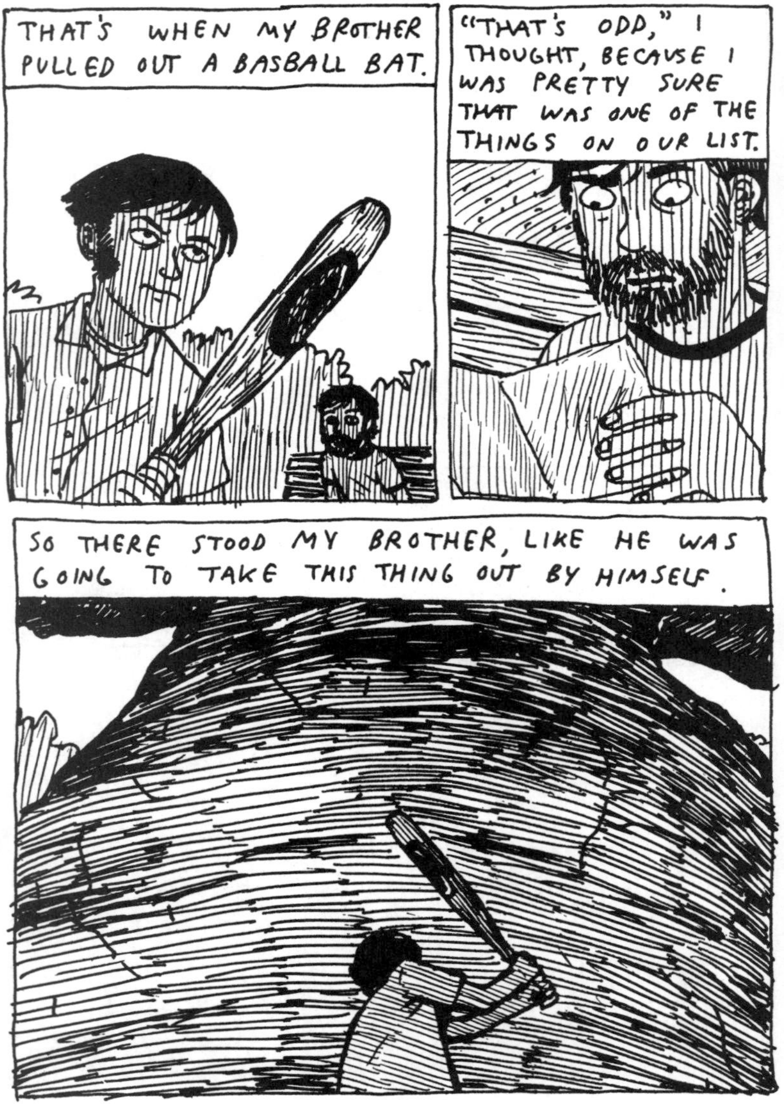
THAT'S WHEN MY BROTHER PULLED OUT A BASBALL BAT.
"THAT'S ODD," I THOUGHT, BECAUSE I WAS PRETTY SURE THAT WAS ONE OF THE THINGS ON OUR LIST.
SO THERE STOOD MY BROTHER, LIKE HE WAS GOING TO TAKE THIS THING OUT BY HIMSELF.

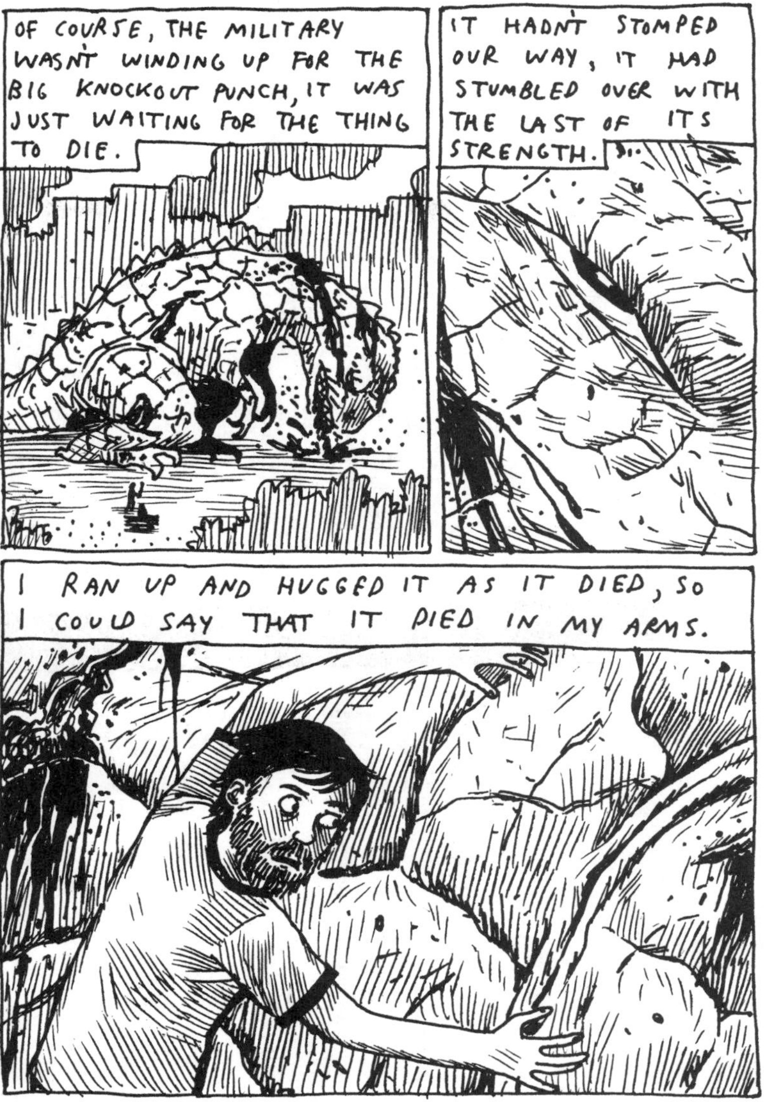
OF COURSE, THE MILITARY WASN'T WINDING UP FOR THE BIG KNOCKOUT PUNCH, IT WAS JUST WAITING FOR THE THING TO DIE.
IT HADN'T STOMPED OUR WAY, IT HAD STUMBLED OVER WITH THE LAST OF ITS STRENGTH.
I RAN UP AND HUGGED IT AS IT DIED, SO I COULD SAY THAT IT DIED IN MY ARMS.

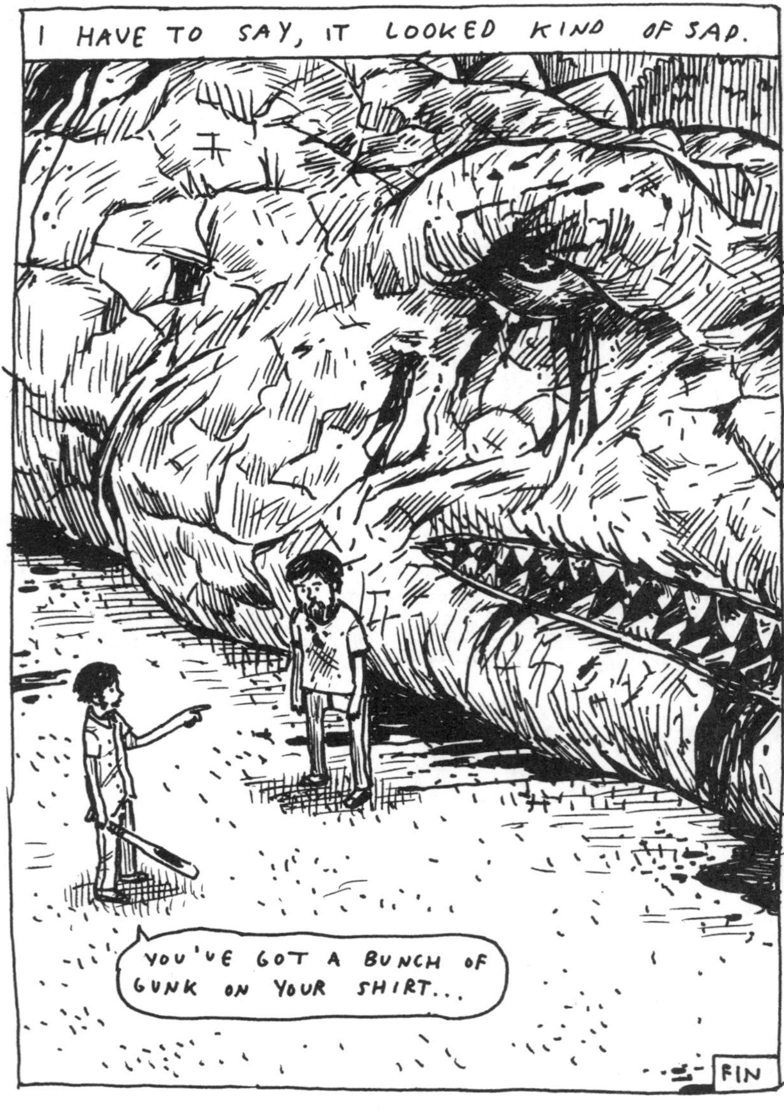
I HAVE TO SAY, IT LOOKED KIND OF SAD.
YOU'VE GOT A BUNCH OF GUNK ON YOUR SHIRT...
FIN

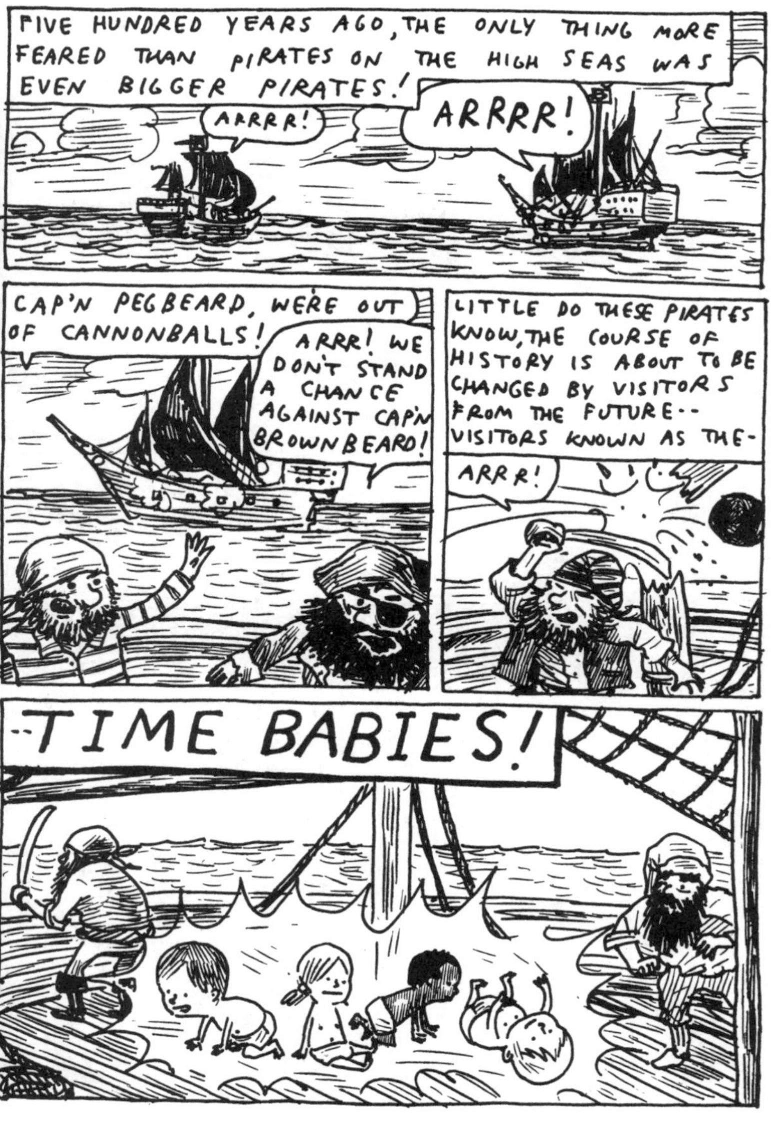
FIVE HUNDRED YEARS AGO, THE ONLY THING MORE FEARED THAN PIRATES ON THE HIGH SEAS WAS EVEN BIGGER PIRATES!
ARRRR!
ARRRRR!
CAP'N PEGBEARD, WE'RE OUT OF CANNONBALLS!
ARRR! WE DON'T STAND A CHANCE AGAINST CAP'N BROWNBEARD!
LITTLE DO THESE PIRATES KNOW, THE COURSE OF HISTORY IS ABOUT TO BE CHANGED BY VISITORS FROM THE FUTURE-- VISITORS KNOWN AS THE-
ARRR!
--TIME BABIES!

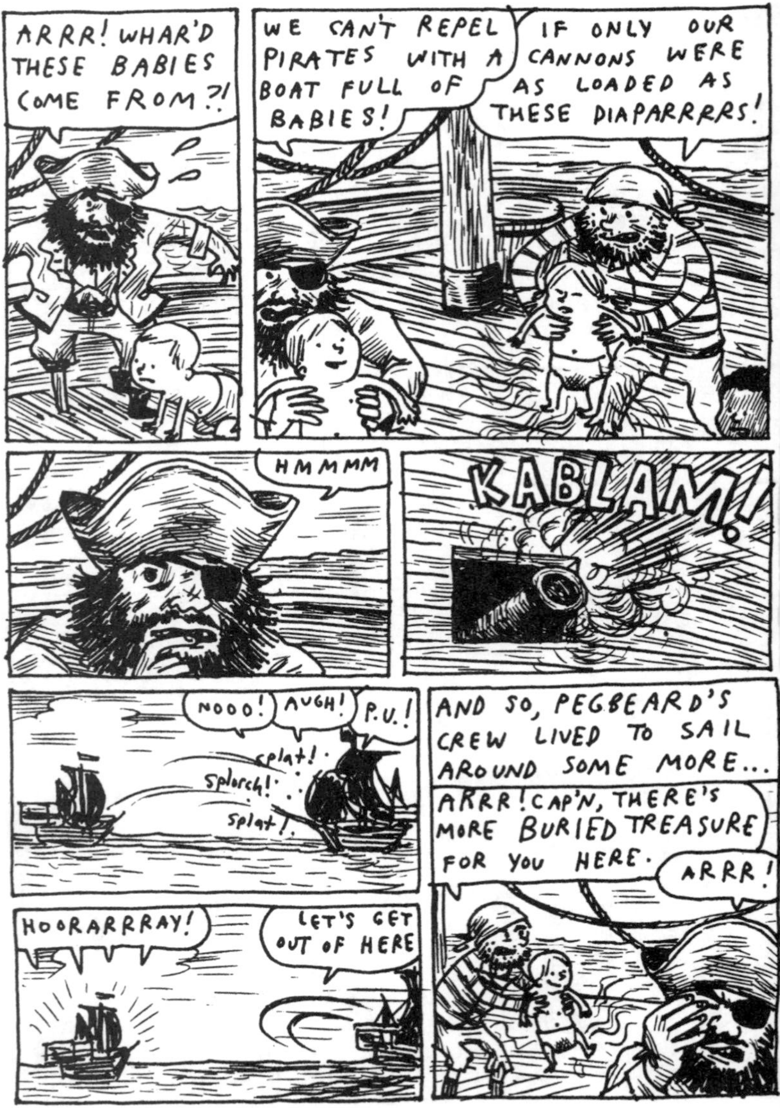
ARRR! WHAR'D THESE BABIES COME FROM?!
WE CAN'T REPEL PIRATES WITH A BOAT FULL OF BABIES!
IF ONLY OUR CANNONS WERE AS LOADED AS THESE DIAPARRRRS!
HMMMM
KABLAM!
NOOO!
AUGH!
P.U.!
splat!
splorch!
splat!
AND SO, PEGBEARD'S CREW LIVED TO SAIL AROUND SOME MORE...
ARRR! CAP'N, THERE'S MORE BURIED TREASURE FOR YOU HERE.
ARRR!
HOORARRRAY!
LET'S GET OUT OF HERE